Simply Tolstoy

Simply Tolstoy

DONNA TUSSING ORWIN

SIMPLY CHARLY
NEW YORK

Copyright © 2017 by Donna Tussing Orwin

Cover Illustration by José Ramos
Cover Design by Scarlett Rugers

All rights reserved. No part of this publication may be reproduced, distributed, or transmitted in any form or by any means, including photocopying, recording, or other electronic or mechanical methods, without the prior written permission of the publisher, except in the case of brief quotations embodied in critical reviews and certain other noncommercial uses permitted by copyright law. For permission requests, write to the publisher at the address below.

permissions@simplycharly.com

ISBN: 978-1-943657-16-2

Brought to you by http://simplycharly.com

To Thanina and Hannah

Contents

	Praise for *Simply Tolstoy*	ix
	Other *Great Lives*	xi
	Series Editor's Foreword	xii
	Preface	xiii
1.	Early Life	1
2.	*War and Peace* and the 1860s	27
3.	The 1870s and *Anna Karenina*	44
4.	A Midlife Crisis	57
5.	A New Path	78
6.	Tolstoy as Guru and Man in Later Life	95
7.	Art and Aesthetics in the Late Period	108
8.	Conclusion and Legacy	114
	Sources	119
	Suggested Reading	120
	About the Author	125
	A Word from the Publisher	126

Praise for *Simply Tolstoy*

"No title could better suit Donna Orwin's wise and riveting biography than *Simply Tolstoy*. For the actual man was contradictory and immensely complex; he only dreamed of simplicity. On this massive life, the erudite and compassionate Orwin trains a meticulous lens that keeps out none of the dark but lets through all the light."

–**Caryl Emerson, A. Watson Armour III University Professor Emeritus of Slavic Languages and Literatures, Princeton University**

"This is a little gem, the best introduction to Tolstoy I have ever encountered, and it is more than that. The most accomplished scholar will find important new insights, the sort that one immediately recognizes as both true and profound. Orwin brings Tolstoy to life as a person and as a writer, and she also shows beautifully how the two are linked. The discussions of Tolstoy's views on psychology and the nature of art are especially illuminating."

–**Gary Saul Morson, Lawrence B. Dumas Professor of the Arts and Humanities and Professor of Slavic Languages and Literatures, Northwestern University**

"Tolstoy's life, work, and thought in 100 pages? It can't be done! But in *Simply Tolstoy*, Donna Orwin does it. Providing concise overviews of Tolstoy's most important literary work in the context of his biography and intellectual historical background, this brief book will appeal to a wide range of readers curious to understand Russia's great novelist and thinker."

–**Andrew Wachtel, President, American University of Central Asia**

"Donna Tussing Orwin's *Simply Tolstoy* is both a personal essay and fact-packed critical biography of Tolstoy. Readers are fortunate that Orwin, one of the foremost scholars of Tolstoy, distills her knowledge into an accessible encounter with this giant. She describes her youthful curiosity about Tolstoy's sincerity and moral goals, concluding that he was a post-Kantian romantic 'who relied on feeling rather than reason for access to . . . truth,' and a pacifist who was the 'greatest war writer of modern times.' Orwin shows how Tolstoy's estate Yasnaya Polyana, 'his little homeland,' shaped his experience. Reading *War and Peace* as a 'founding myth of modern Russia,' she argues that war is its dominant theme. 'Horrible as it is, war has its charm.' *Simply Tolstoy* raises questions relevant today, about war, marriage, intimacy, or how to live a moral life, questions that play out against the canvas of actuality: 'No author,' writes Orwin, 'has more thoroughly recreated the interplay between circumstance and free choice than Tolstoy.'"

—**Robin Feuer Miller, Edytha Macy Gross Professor of Humanities, Brandeis University**

"This engaging and readable little work is an introduction worthy of the master. Donna Orwin, the foremost Western Tolstoy scholar, has spent a lifetime immersed in the writer's works. She brings to the task a formidable knowledge of philosophy, Russian literature, and history, and biting, critical intelligence. Authoritative, thorough, and stimulating, this book brims with original insights that seasoned readers, as well as Tolstoy's novices, will appreciate. Take a couple of hours, curl up under your beach umbrella, and read *Simply Tolstoy*. Then go back and read your Tolstoy, with this powerful little book at your elbow."

—**Carol Apollonio, Professor of the Practice of Slavic and Eurasian Studies, Duke University**

Other *Great Lives*

Simply Austen by Joan Klingel Ray
Simply Beckett by Katherine Weiss
Simply Beethoven by Leon Plantinga
Simply Chekhov by Carol Apollonio
Simply Chomsky by Raphael Salkie
Simply Chopin by William Smialek
Simply Darwin by Michael Ruse
Simply Descartes by Kurt Smith
Simply Dickens by Paul Schlicke
Simply Dirac by Helge Kragh
Simply Einstein by Jimena Canales
Simply Eliot by Joseph Maddrey
Simply Euler by Robert E. Bradley
Simply Faulkner by Philip Weinstein
Simply Fitzgerald by Kim Moreland
Simply Freud by Stephen Frosh
Simply Gödel by Richard Tieszen
Simply Hegel by Robert L. Wicks
Simply Hitchcock by David Sterritt
Simply Joyce by Margot Norris
Simply Machiavelli by Robert Fredona
Simply Napoleon by J. David Markham & Matthew Zarzeczny
Simply Nietzsche by Peter Kail
Simply Proust by Jack Jordan
Simply Riemann by Jeremy Gray
Simply Sartre by David Detmer
Simply Stravinsky by Pieter van den Toorn
Simply Turing by Michael Olinick
Simply Wagner by Thomas S. Grey
Simply Wittgenstein by James C. Klagge

Series Editor's Foreword

Simply Charly's "Great Lives" series offers brief but authoritative introductions to the world's most influential people—scientists, artists, writers, economists, and other historical figures whose contributions have had a meaningful and enduring impact on our society.

Each book provides an illuminating look at the works, ideas, personal lives, and the legacies these individuals left behind, also shedding light on the thought processes, specific events, and experiences that led these remarkable people to their groundbreaking discoveries or other achievements. Additionally, every volume explores various challenges they had to face and overcome to make history in their respective fields, as well as the little-known character traits, quirks, strengths, and frailties, myths, and controversies that sometimes surrounded these personalities.

Our authors are prominent scholars and other top experts who have dedicated their careers to exploring each facet of their subjects' work and personal lives.

Unlike many other works that are merely descriptions of the major milestones in a person's life, the "Great Lives" series goes above and beyond the standard format and content. It brings substance, depth, and clarity to the sometimes-complex lives and works of history's most powerful and influential people.

We hope that by exploring this series, readers will not only gain new knowledge and understanding of what drove these geniuses, but also find inspiration for their own lives. Isn't this what a great book is supposed to do?

Charles Carlini, Simply Charly
New York City

Preface

Leo (Lev) Tolstoy is one of the world's most famous writers. His works have been translated into over 60 languages, including Arabic, Albanian, Afrikaans, Armenian, Azerbaijani, Basque, Belarusian, Bengali, Bulgarian, Burmese (Myanmar language), Catalan, Chinese, Chuvash, Croatian, Czech, Danish, Dutch, Esperanto, Estonian, Finnish, French, Italian, German, Greek, Gujarati, Ha, Hebrew, Hindi, Hungarian, Icelandic, Indonesian, Japanese, Kannada, Korean, Kurdish, Kyrgyz, Latvian, Lithuanian, Macedonian, Malayalam, Marathi, Mongolian, Norwegian, Pashto, Persian, Polish, Portuguese, Punjabi, Romanian, Serbian, Sinhalese, Slovak, Slovenian, Sorbian, Spanish, Swedish, Tamil, Telugu, Thai, Turkish, Ukrainian, Urdu, Uzbek, Welsh, and Yiddish.

There have been 13 translations of the novel *Anna Karenina* into English alone, and nine of them are still in print. Two early translations are also available as print-on-demand publications. *War and Peace* has 12 translations, plus two substantial revisions of previous translations. Seven of those are still in print, and four early translations available as print-on-demand publications. There have been 16 translations of *The Death of Ivan Ilych*, with 10 still in print, and three early ones available as print-on-demand publications.

Tolstoy was more than a writer of fiction. In his lifetime and beyond, he inspired social and political change. Though he died before the Russian Revolution of 1917, in his later life he contributed to the delegitimization of the Tsarist regime, and, as we shall see, his influence spread far beyond Russian borders.

I became attracted to Tolstoy when, as a student, I discovered in his diaries that he had struggled in his youth with the same questions and problems I had, and he investigated them with a sincerity that I admired. In my long career, I haven't found answers to all my questions, in his writing or elsewhere, but he still fascinates me. I wanted to know the relationship between that sincerity and his moral goals, and that is one of the overarching themes in this book. This first question led me to many others, some of which I elaborate on. It is not an exaggeration to say that characters from his fiction have become constant presences in my life, companions whose life stories have guided me in my own. Even when, as happens from time to time, Tolstoy infuriates me, I find myself reconnecting with him through his works. I feel privileged and humbled to have such a great man as a mentor. My bond with him and his art is an example of how great authors can influence individuals and societies distant from them in time and space.

Tolstoy lived until age 82, and he was a prolific writer. Even the 90-volume iconic Jubilee Edition (1928–1958) of his collected works, which includes diaries and letters, does not contain all his writings. A new 120-volume Academy of Sciences Edition is planned at the time of this writing. So, obviously, this book cannot cover all his life experiences or everything he wrote.

In choosing what to include and how to balance all the different facets of the man and his art, I have relied on the chronology I prepared for *The Cambridge Companion to Tolstoy* (2002). I have also borrowed from my own earlier writings. I have tried to give a thorough account of his fiction and nonfiction writings and to show how his art and ideas stayed the same and yet changed over time. I have drawn upon biography, psychology, philosophy, and history to show how these factors work together or against one another to produce the inimitable Tolstoy. This book is my own overview, but I am indebted to the numerous scholars whom I have read as I studied Tolstoy. I am also grateful to Tim Klähn, Michael Denner, Ken Lantz, Clifford Orwin, Edith Klein, and the editors of *Simply Charly* for their help in shaping the final manuscript. My goal is to provide an introduction to the whole man and his writings so that readers can engage with whatever aspect interests them.

Donna Tussing Orwin
Toronto, Canada

1. Early Life

Family

Family in Russia has special significance. In a country where, to this day, institutions don't have much power and the rule of law does not always prevail, people depend more on family for networks and support. An interesting proof of the importance of family in Russian culture is that peoples' full names include mention of their fathers. Tolstoy's name was Lev Nikolayevich Tolstoy, with Nikolayevich a so-called patronymic meaning "son of Nikolay." Russians also rely on outstanding individuals rather than governments to bring about change. Tolstoy used family connections throughout his life, from the time he was trying to establish himself in the army to later years when he needed help with his various projects. He came from nobility and felt a keen responsibility to serve the country in some way appropriate to the high social status he had inherited but not personally earned. Tolstoy would have learned about his ancestors from family lore, which often differed from what we now know or surmise. When he wrote about those ancestors in whom he was particularly interested—he did so rarely—he left out details that he probably knew but did not want to share with the general public.

Tolstoy's prototype for Prince Nikolay Bolkonsky in *War and Peace* was his maternal grandfather, Nikolay Sergeyevich Volkonsky (1753-1821). He came from a clan of princes said to be descended from Riurik, the mythical 9th-century founder of Kievan Rus, Russia's predecessor which endured from the 9th to the early 13th century. His life story illustrates the situation of an aristocrat in his day—highly privileged but uncertain.

Prince Volkonsky distinguished himself under Tsarina Catherine the Great, first as an officer in the Turkish campaign of 1780, and after a successful career in the army, as a diplomat. Catherine wanted him to marry the mistress (and supposedly niece) of Prince Grigori Potyomkin. Volkonsky refused, saying, "What made him think I should marry his whore?" Under the rule of Catherine's son, Paul, he was dismissed from the army in 1797 for failing to appear at a review, but was readmitted after 18 months. He retired in 1799 to his estate at Yasnaya Polyana, a property in the fertile heartland of Russia 120 miles south of Moscow that his father had acquired in 1763. In the final two decades of his life, Nikolay Sergeyevich planned and mostly completed the building of a two-story, 32-room mansion with surrounding outbuildings and landscaping. He also amassed a great book collection that nurtured his grandson and forms the basis of the Yasnaya Polyana library to this day.

Though he never met him (having been born seven years after Nikolay Sergeyevich's death), Tolstoy greatly admired his grandfather for his independence, feistiness, intelligence, pride, and aesthetic sense. He must have noticed from a portrait that hung on the wall of the salon at Yasnaya Polyana that he had inherited old Volkonsky's black eyebrows and piercing gray eyes. (His own 1873 portrait by Ivan Kramskoy that hangs across from it seems to emphasize the similarity between the two.) He may have had the prince in mind in 1844, when he enrolled in the faculty of Oriental languages at Kazan University, intending to become a diplomat, and also in the 1850s, when he joined the army and contemplated a military career. Tolstoy lived almost his entire life at Yasnaya Polyana, which in its overall geometrical design and simplicity expressed the 18th-century taste and mentality of his grandfather. He was born there and as the youngest son—there was no right of succession for the first-born child among the Russian nobility—he inherited the family's principal residence. At first, he seemed not sufficiently to appreciate or care for the estate. In 1854, he instructed his sister's husband to sell the main house, where he had been born, to pay off gambling debts. (It was bought by a neighboring landowner, dismantled, moved, and reconstructed in a village 20 miles away. It survived until the 1920s when it burnt down.) By 1858, however, in an unfinished work entitled *Summer in the Village*, that explores relations between peasants and their masters, he called his estate "my little homeland." He wrote there that "without my Yasnaya Polyana, it is hard for me to contemplate Russia and my relation to her. Without Yasnaya Polyana, I can perhaps more clearly see the general laws necessary for my fatherland, but I will not be able to love it to distraction." In the often-arbitrary world of Russian autocracy, Yasnaya Polyana became a private, inviolable space, the expression of the freedom and dignity of a Russian nobleman.

When Prince Nikolay Sergeyevich had retired to Yasnaya Polyana in 1799, he also tended to the upbringing of his beloved only child (and Tolstoy's mother), Princess Marya Nikolayevna, who was born in 1790. She must have been one of the most educated Russian women of her generation. Under her father's tutelage, she studied five languages (including Russian, which was unusual for the upper classes, who spoke and wrote mostly in French), mathematics, some science, and classical literature. She was an accomplished pianist and storyteller, as well as an author of prose and poetry. Most important to Tolstoy was her good character, which combined modesty, magnanimity, and a sense of social justice. According to his *Reminiscences*, she had four great loves in her life: Prince Lev Golitsyn, who died before they could marry and after whom she named her youngest son; a French companion, Mademoiselle Hénissienne; her oldest son Nikolay; and Tolstoy himself, once Nikolay had graduated to the care of male tutors. After her marriage to Nikolay Ilyich Tolstoy in 1822, which was happy though not a love match, she devoted herself to raising her children.

The Tolstoy clan fancifully traced its origins to a nobleman named Indris, who supposedly traveled from Lithuania or some other part of the Holy Roman Empire with his two sons and 3,000 followers and arrived in the principality of Chernigov in 1353. The Tolstoys were known for their intelligence, their long lives, and their love of women. Tolstoy's ancestor Pyotr Andreyevich Tolstoy (1645–1729) was elevated to the rank of count in 1724, under Tsar Peter I (the

Great). He was a very capable man, traveling abroad in the tsar's service, learning Italian, and serving as ambassador to Constantinople. He was hard and morally dubious. Tolstoy, who studied the Petrine era in detail while considering writing a book about it in the 1870s, certainly knew that Pyotr Andreyevich had helped Tsar Peter lure his son Aleksey back to Russia and to his death. Peter said of him when he was already 80 years old, "Pyotr Andreyevich is in every way a very able man, but it is just as well when you have dealings with him to keep a stone in your pocket to break his teeth in case he decides to bite you!" Pyotr Andreyevich lost his title in 1727, when he fell into disgrace after having taken the wrong side in machinations following Peter's death. (The title was restored to the family in 1760.) When Tolstoy was asked to provide a biography of his family (published in 1879), he traced the Tolstoy line back to this ancestor, identifying him only as "an associate of Peter the Great." This was indicative of the importance that Tolstoy placed on family and of his reluctance to air its dirty linen.

Tolstoy's paternal grandfather, Count Ilya Andreyevich Tolstoy (1757–1820), was a warm-hearted, fun-loving, and impractical man, who had squandered his own fortune, so he spent his wealthy wife's money and at the end of his life had to take a job as the governor of Kazan province. Accused of "irregularities" in the performance of his duties, he lost that position after five years and died soon afterward. Though Tolstoy could not regard this grandfather as a role model, he did defend him as an honorable man, and he admired his "trusting" nature, so different from his own keen, proud, reserved, and analytical one. Tolstoy did not mention in *Reminiscences* that Ilya Andreyevich was dismissed as Kazan's governor, and in his few words about the governor's position, Tolstoy implicitly defended him as honest. The portrait of this grandfather also hung in the salon at Yasnaya Polyana, and he was the prototype for Count Rostov in *War and Peace*.

Tolstoy's father, Count Nikolay Ilyich, was born in 1794. He joined the army in 1812 when Napoleon invaded Russia. He fought in Germany in 1813, was eventually captured by the French, and was taken to Paris. He was liberated when the Allies took the city in 1814. He left the army in 1819 and entered civil service. Nikolay's father's estate was so encumbered with debt that he did not accept his inheritance when his father died, but he had to find a way to support his mother in the style to which she was accustomed. In 1824, he retired to his wife's estate of Yasnaya Polyana and spent the rest of his life running it. Tolstoy said that although his father did not do this especially well (unlike his maternal grandfather), he was an unusually kind landowner who never mistreated his serfs. He also explained that his father and his circle of friends were "free people" who did not kowtow to the government of the day, and even allowed themselves to criticize it. The family had no civil servants among their close friends. As Tolstoy wrote late in life, even as a child, he "understood that my father humbled himself before no one and never altered his bold, merry, and often ironic tone. And this sense of personal dignity that I saw in him increased my love, my adoration of him."

Childhood

Tolstoy himself was born on August 28, 1828. It tells us something about his personality and the way he saw patterns everywhere that he always regarded his birth date, and especially the number 28, as lucky. His mother died in 1830 when his sister Marya was five months old.

His older brothers Nikolay, Dmitri, and Sergey, had been born in 1823, 1826, and 1827, respectively. Left a widower with five young children, his father proposed marriage to a distant relative, Tatyana Aleksandrovna Yorgolskaya. She declined his offer but raised the Tolstoy children nevertheless. When Count Nikolay died suddenly in 1837, his sister, Countess Aleksandra Ilynichna Osten-Saken, became the children's official guardian, while Tatyana remained responsible for their care. Countess Aleksandra died in 1841, and her sister,

Countess Pelageya Ilynichna Yushkova, took over the guardianship, and Tatyana went to live with a sister. Tolstoy spent the first eight years of his life at Yasnaya Polyana. In 1836, while still summering there, the family moved to Moscow to prepare the eldest son, Nikolay, for university. In 1841, they moved to Kazan, a port city 200 miles east of Moscow on the Volga River, to live with Countess Pelageya and her landowner husband.

All this could have been the making of a Dickensian (or Dostoevskian) melodrama, with relatives, crooked lawyers, and bureaucrats robbing the orphaned Tolstoys. But that is not what happened. Though there were some family tensions, Tatyana Yorgolskaya looked after the children lovingly, and the guardians conscientiously oversaw their money and property. Both Yorgolskaya–"Auntie" as Tolstoy called her–and Countess Pelageya ended their days as honored elders at Yasnaya Polyana. And when it came time to divide the inheritance among the children, there is no record of their having squabbled amongst themselves over their shares.

Tolstoy's nickname was "Lyova-ryova" [Crybaby Lev]. His sister remembered him as a sunny, very impressionable child who loved to joke and cried easily when his brothers teased him. He was also very imaginative; at around age 8, he injured himself by leaping from a window six feet from the ground in an attempt to fly. The effects of these qualities are on display in two autobiographical fragments that Tolstoy wrote, one in 1878 (*My Life*) and the other one (*Reminiscences*) from 1903–06. In both, he vividly describes individual moments of his early life. All these descriptions include detailed accounts of his own feelings: how much he loved someone ("Auntie," for instance, or his father) or how he wept or wondered. Therefore, even when he wrote about others–the adults who cared for him, his siblings, or his servants–the text is also about him, and he comes across as extraordinarily sensitive.

The ingredients of an artistic temperament were evidently present from an early age. In *My Life*, he confessed that as a young child his dreams and daytime musings were similar. It is also very clear that he made up the first two stories in *Reminiscences*: one about being swaddled and the other about being bathed as an infant. In fact, he could not have remembered such early events. Many of the recollections in the second, longer fragment are recognizable as having been written into works of fiction. The description of the father in *Childhood*, for instance, uses many details recorded in *Reminiscences*. And in *War and Peace*, Tolstoy recreated at the Rostov country estate his own memories of Christmas festivities and masked actors. But in his mind, reminiscences jumbled together with figments of imagination in a way that makes it impossible to distinguish them without corroborating evidence that something he "remembered" really happened. There is very little such evidence from his early life.

In both autobiographical fragments, Tolstoy complained that he couldn't link the moments he remembered into a coherent chain of cause and effect. As he put it in *Reminiscences*, he could not write a full biography because of his inability to connect individual "events and states of mind." This is a very important clue about how he mined his own life to construct fiction and, in some cases, nonfiction. Imagination is needed to join "memories" together, and those memories can be placed in different sequences, set within different frameworks, and serve different purposes. Depending on those purposes, Tolstoy could employ different memories. A significant example of this is the use he made of the famous anecdote of the green stick. At around age 10, Tolstoy's oldest brother, Nikolay, supposedly told his younger siblings that a green stick buried close to a ravine in the woods near the house at Yasnaya Polyana had the secret of human happiness written on it. Tolstoy's grave, as he requested, is near this place. He recounted this anecdote in *Reminiscences*, and his son Ilya wrote in his memoirs, published in 1914, that his father often related it to him and his siblings. It advanced an ideal of universal brotherhood especially dear to him at that time, one that he wanted his biography to support. Given the importance he ascribed late in his life to this memory, it is surely significant that, so far as I know, he did not mention it in any of his writings before then. There is no reason to think that the anecdote is not true, however. Tolstoy treated his memories as a bank of insights into the realities of inner life that preceded any conclusions about that life, but that he could use in the service of such conclusions.

Like everyone, Tolstoy was shaped by his life and times. The early loss of his parents was the definitive event of his own life. His first book, *Childhood*, is about the death of the protagonist's mother. Having lost his own mother so early, Tolstoy could not remember her, and therefore he was free to imagine her as perfect. Significantly, the father in *Childhood* is loved and loving, but flawed. Tolstoy did not idealize his father, whom he lost when he was eight, the way he did his mother. The relationship he imagined with her arguably became a model for an intimacy he longed for his entire life but never achieved.

This hunger for intimacy was a driving force behind his desire to write fiction. From the beginning, he imagined his "perfect reader" (whom he actually defined and addressed in drafts of *Childhood*). This ideal reader would be perfectly in harmony with him, the author. In that sense, all his art is a confession to this reader, and it is no accident that Jean-Jacques Rousseau's *Confessions* had, in Tolstoy's own words, an "enormous" effect on him. The first draft of what became *Childhood* identifies his reader as his "confessor," and, paraphrasing Rousseau from his *Confessions*, presents the narrator as imperfect but worthy because, unlike others, he sincerely confesses his faults.

In 1851, quoting Nikolay Gogol (the greatest writer of the previous generation) that his last work, *Selected Passages from Correspondence with Friends*, had "sung itself out of my soul," Tolstoy wrote that all good compositions are created this way. This romantic mantra became the basis of his definition of art—expressed in his book, *What Is Art?*—as an infection by the artist's feelings of another. His need for intimacy with his reader helps explain why Tolstoy could not give up fiction even, as occasionally happened, he very much wanted to do so.

University

At Kazan University, Tolstoy was not a motivated student. He lacked purpose and discipline, showing up late for some classes and skipping others. Having failed his exams in Oriental languages, he transferred to the faculty of law rather than repeat his first year. He left the university in 1847 without graduating. While at university, he participated in Kazan's society life, both high and low, managing to contract a venereal disease for the first, but not the last time. But he also began the intellectual and spiritual journey there that continued his whole life. It was not driven by idle curiosity, but by need: he had started to ponder how he should live his life. This may have happened when he entered university or perhaps a little earlier.

As he put it in a passage from *The Cossacks* (1863), which draws upon his life in the late 1840s and early 1850s, to describe the state of mind of the novella's hero Olenin, "[h]e meditated on the use to which he should devote that force of youth present in a man once in a lifetime: not the force of mind, heart, or education, but that unrepeatable surge, that power given a man only once to make himself, or even—as it seemed to him—to make the universe, into anything he wishes: should it be to art, to science, to love of woman, or to practical activities?" Already in this passage, we see that Tolstoy doubts the efficacy of social rather than individual reform, but as a young man, he contemplated a life of good works within every traditional career path open to a nobleman: diplomacy, the civil service, management of his estate with its 300 serfs, and the military. He wanted to pursue one of these "to make the universe into anything he wished."

The word "science" [*nauka*] in Russian has a broader meaning than in English, and the "science" Tolstoy studied was philosophy, most especially the writings of Rousseau and another French philosopher, Montesquieu. He read the latter as part of his first musings on justice, politics, and his civic responsibilities. With this in mind and, no doubt, with an eye to working in government, he started a comparison of Catherine the Great's *Instruction* (a document meant to guide legal reform in Russia) and Montesquieu's great book of political theory *Spirit of the Laws*. But Rousseau was the dominant influence on his early thought. In his treatise *Émile, On Education*, Tolstoy discovered a guide for understanding and regulating his personal life. Another Rousseau work, the novel *Julie, or The New Heloise*, influenced his ideas about women and love. Further, *The First Discourse* (on the arts and sciences) and *The Second Discourse* (on the origins of inequality) shaped his perspective on civilization. One summer at Yasnaya Polyana during his university years, Tolstoy even adopted a simplified Rousseauian lifestyle, sleeping in the same garment he wore during the day. He read Rousseau's entire oeuvre, as he recalled in 1901, "even the *Music Dictionary* [*Dictionnaire de musique*]," and "many of his pages are so close to me that it seems to me that I wrote them myself." The use of the present tense in this statement testifies to the enduring influence of the philosopher on him.

A precipitating factor in the launching of Tolstoy's spiritual quest may have been his first crisis of faith. He related in *Confession* (to be discussed further below) that a friend told him and his brothers in 1838 that God did not exist, and that by the time he left university at 18, he believed only in a cult of "self-perfectivization." It is clear from his first diaries that he felt he would have to get his "soul" (as Russians call the inner life) in order, but he couldn't do that without understanding its makeup, so he set about studying it.

He drew two philosophical conclusions that shaped his understanding of human psychology ever after. He implicitly agreed with the early modern philosopher Descartes (whom he had not read in university, but learned about later) that "I think, therefore I am." Human beings are unique because they alone among animals are self-conscious and therefore have the ability to distance themselves from their actions and reflect on them. Without self-consciousness, psychological realism, of which Tolstoy became one of the greatest practitioners and innovators, would be impossible, because he could not have mined his inner life to construct his prose. But the young philosopher also disagreed with Descartes in a very important way by observing that to think one has to want to do so. Therefore, he concluded, desire, or will, precedes reason in the soul, and to understand human beings we must understand desire and will too. The soul is multifaceted, composed of body, feelings, mind and will, and a good, moral life depends on the proper interaction of these elements.

Such a life turned out to be difficult, not because the young Tolstoy was a bad person but because ordering his youthful energies was not easy. A "Franklin journal," as he named it, that he started in 1847, brims with plans and resolutions, and contains a rueful record of his failures to fulfill them. He was passionate, willful, moral, spiritual, and thoughtful all at the same time. These complexities—they were what fascinated me about him when I read his diaries in college—turned out to be a significant trigger of his genius as a writer. He failed to get himself in hand, but as he struggled futilely to do so, he acquired an immense and subtle understanding of human psychology.

Tolstoy Becomes a Writer

In the 1840s and earlier, Tolstoy read fiction, both Russian and foreign, but there is no indication that he himself was intending to write. He loved music and, perhaps influenced by Rousseau, he plunged into the study of it, began writing articles about it, and intensively practiced the piano. In his 1852 diary, he remembered the "happiness of the artist" that he had experienced in the summer of 1850. In December of that year, he recorded working on a story, and around that time he began what became the first redaction of *Childhood*. Diary entries and other fragments from that year teem with an interest in writing fiction.

There is no question that the fiction developed out of his diary and notebooks from 1847–51: his interest in the workings of his inner life, his analysis of it, his attempts to govern it through rules, and the records of his failures to do so. The great Soviet Tolstoy scholar Boris Eikhenbaum suggested in his book *The Young Tolstoy* that all this hard work was really the creation of "a methodology of self-observation," creating the bits out of which he constructed his psychological prose. According to Eikhenbaum, he accomplished this by interrupting and thereby distorting the flow of his own inner life. It is certainly true that, around 1850, Tolstoy realized the potential for art in his earlier writings.

In 1851, he translated from English (with the help of a French translation) a portion of Laurence Sterne's 1768 novel, A *Sentimental Journey Through France and Italy*, and also started an untitled work that we now call A *History of Yesterday*. These two undertakings may be linked as an attempt—doomed to fail—to transcribe the inner life of the first-person protagonist of A *History of Yester*day in the spirit of Sterne's *The Life and Opinions of Tristram Shandy, Gentleman*, and as a chance to practice the voice of a narrator of such a project. Eikhenbaum's brilliant insight about the contribution of the diaries simplifies what was going on, however. One fragment from 1851—*Why Do People Write?*—suggests another connection between Tolstoy's self-help efforts and fiction. He argued there that people desire happiness above all else and that it is virtue that confers the greatest happiness. Therefore, only writings that teach virtue are worthwhile, and those would be the morally instructive and philosophical works that he was reading and even trying to write himself. "But," he corrected himself, "aren't books useful that, depicting virtue artistically, act as models?" Around the very same time, he contemplated writing a novel about the life of Auntie Yorgolskaya, who would model virtue. A year later he reported in his diary working on a "dogmatic" (by which he meant positive) "novel of a Russian landowner." However, he did not write either novel. Instead, he chose another approach mentioned in the same diary entry, exemplified by what he called *Four Stages of Development*, which would "constitute my novel up to Tiflis [Tbilisi, Georgia, where he had recently moved]. I can write about it because it is far from me. And as the novel of a person who is intelligent, sensitive and erring, it will be instructive, though not dogmatic."

Both Rousseau's *Confessions* and *Julie, or The New Heloise* would serve as templates for such a work. At this point, Tolstoy had already published *Childhood* and was working on the next installment of *Four Stages*, called *Adolescence*, which was published in 1854. He eventually published a third, *Youth*, in 1857. All three works, which came to be called his autobiographical trilogy, mined his diaries for the methodology of psychological analysis developed there, and also for raw data. All three contain central chapters that define the stage they depict, and, to some extent, each of them is structured around that definition. All, but especially *Childhood*, comprise a new genre in Russian literature, which author Andrew Wachtel called, in *The Battle for Childhood: Creation of a Russian Myth*, pseudo-biography, combining "the immediacy of autobiography with the creative freedom of the novel."

Childhood

The plot of this book takes place on the country estate of the first-person narrator, Nikolenka, and in Moscow where he moves with his father and brothers. Tolstoy built his work partly on a Rousseauian comparison between rural and urban life, and the negative effects of the latter on the psyche. Even in the country part of the novella, however, the pure state of childhood is already past (though it still lingers in enticing ways).

The work begins with portents of the death of the mother, which occurs at its end. This brings an end to childhood, with its complete intimacy between child and mother, though that intimacy is already on its way to destruction in the work's opening scene. There, Nikolenka, caught in an embarrassing confusion of hubristic and touching feelings, weeps and then explains his tears as a response to a false dream that his mother has died. Young children, as Tolstoy conceives them, live completely in the moment and without self-reflection or duplicity. The development of a sense of self—and the need to justify its coherence to oneself and others—is fatal to pure childishness as Tolstoy understood it, and, therefore, fatal to the possibility of any sustained intimacy. The latter requires a complete openness impossible once the self retreats behind defensive walls as Nikolenka does in this scene.

Interestingly, in both country and city, Tolstoy associated the end of childhood with problems of authorship. The narrator makes up a story to cover his shame in Chapter 1, and later, in Chapter 16, he feels guilty for writing a poem for his grandmother's birthday celebration in which, to make a rhyme, he claims to love her more than his mother. Writing is shown in this case as a step away from complete transparency of the self. At its purest, art should not be like this. As Tolstoy explained in a draft of *Childhood* entitled *To Readers*, it is musical, not analytical, and connects the author with his reader so that "every note in my heart sounds in his."

The success of *Childhood* determined the ambitious young author's choice of profession. He confessed much later to his wife that, reading the positive reviews, he had felt "tears of joy." When his siblings Marya and Sergey read it, they immediately recognized themselves in it, but didn't guess that the pseudonymous author L.N. was their own brother. The public loved the book because it portrayed a gentry childhood both realistically and idealistically at the same time. After the publication of *Adolescence*, Ivan Turgenev, author of *A Sportsman's Sketches* and the most famous author of the day, called Tolstoy "the successor to Gogol" (who at the time was admired as a realist), but "not at all like him." With its combination of psychological depth and an account of gentry's life in country and city, *Childhood* gave Russian realism a three-dimensionality that it had previously lacked.

Off to War

Tolstoy wrote *Childhood* in the Caucasus region, where he traveled in spring 1851 with his brother Nikolay, an artillery officer home on leave. The Russians had been fighting a war of attrition there for decades, and Tolstoy, disgusted with an idle life and fleeing a gambling habit, decided to start over again in a new setting. It was in the Caucasus that he read the complete works of Plato translated into French by Victor Cousin.

Along with Rousseau, the Greek philosopher became another enduring philosophical influence on Tolstoy's writing. He wrote later that his favorite dialogues were the *Phaedo* and the *Symposium*. The first of these, about death, and the second, about love, would have been connected for him because he believed mortality generates the sense of incompleteness in humans that gives rise to Eros, the need to complete oneself through total intimacy with someone else. The interwoven complications of love in its many forms and death are the deepest themes in Tolstoy's psychological prose.

In January 1852, Tolstoy joined the artillery as a bombardier fourth class, noncommissioned officer stationed in the North Caucasus. In February, in a baptism by fire that he never forgot, he was almost killed in action by a shell that shattered the wheel of a cannon he was aiming. Though he thought many times during his army service about retiring to become a full-time writer, he also seriously considered a military career. He remained in the army until 1857 and fought in the Crimean War (1853–56), first on the Southern Front in Romania and then, starting in November 1854, in Crimea, where he participated on the front lines in the siege of Sevastopol.

War offered Tolstoy a great writing opportunity that he seized with both hands. His first war story, *The Raid*, was written in the Caucasus in 1853 and grew out of his youthful anxiety about courage. It also reflects the early and enduring influence the form of Platonic dialogue had on him, with its mix of narrative and commentary. *The Raid* borrows a definition of courage from Plato's dialogue on courage, the *Laches,* and applies it to the experiences of two characters: the first-person narrator and the veteran officer Captain Khlopov. But Tolstoy turned out to be a brave and, if you believe one memoirist, even foolhardy warrior, and he soon turned his attention to other aspects of the psychology and practice of war.

Tolstoy wrote three sketches from his time in the Crimean city of Sevastopol. The first, *Sevastopol in December* (1855), read like a report from the front and made him famous with a Russian public hungry for news. This sketch located the truth of war in the hospital (not in glorious battle), but it celebrated conscripted Russian soldiers who, having learned this truth firsthand, still fight stubbornly on. The story was welcomed by the government as patriotic, and was immediately republished in the military newspaper *Russian Veteran* and even translated into French and published in Brussels in the official Russian newspaper there, *Le Nord.* The other two sketches were less positive, but certainly Tolstoy's experience defending Russian territory (as opposed to his participation in the offensive wars in the Caucasus) ignited patriotic feelings in him without which he could not have provided a complete account of war in all its aspects in *War and Peace*.

The three Sevastopol sketches were radical experiments in war writing that anticipated his great novel in different ways. The first-person narrator of *Sevastopol in December* transports the reader—addressed as "you"—to the physical site of the siege by building a portrait of it based on an appeal to sense perceptions of sight, hearing, smell, touch, and even temperature. This rhetorical device appears already in *Childhood,* but it is only here that it expands to become part of Tolstoy's strategy for drawing readers into his world. *Sevastopol in May* (1855) explores the psychology of the Russian officer from Tolstoy's own war experience. A stew of feelings—fear of death, love of honor, pride, vanity, raw ambition, love of glory, and a sense of duty—bubbles in various officers and influences their behavior in the chaos of war. The individual soldier doesn't know what is going on even when he is involved, and therefore tends to make up stories after the fact that recount what he thinks should have happened rather than what actually did. This phenomenon of false reporting was one of Tolstoy's great discoveries about war. On the other hand, he went deeper than anyone else had ever done in recounting the experience and feelings of the individual soldier. Most breathtaking are the death agonies of the officer Praskukhin, seen from the dying man's own point of view. There is no single hero in this sketch. Instead, a stern third-person narrator oversees an account of war psychology illustrated in the experiences of various typical officers. Finally, *Sevastopol in August* (1856) tells the story of the Kozeltsov brothers, both artillery officers, one a wounded veteran returning to the battlefield, and the other arriving there directly from cadet school. The background of a more general description of army life in this sketch anticipated *War and Peace*. Both brothers die heroic deaths that—while neither directly influences the outcome of the battle—illustrate Russian courage and, to some extent, its causes. The sketch ends with the retreat from Sevastopol. Tolstoy was there and shared the opinion of many young officers that those on the front lines had fought well but that the army as an organization was corrupt and needed reforming. *Sevastopol in August* concentrates on the stories of two characters rather than, as in *Sevastopol in May*, on episodes in the lives of several. Its more novelistic cast may reflect the fact that Tolstoy was reading novels by writers like William Makepeace Thackeray and Honoré de Balzac at the time.

In addition to the stories just described, Tolstoy wrote or started a number of lesser works about war and soldiers in the 1850s (*The Wood-cutting* [1855] and *Two Hussars* [1856], for instance). *The Cossacks* (1863) is the most important among these, but since it is also a product of the period after Tolstoy resigned from the army, I will treat it later on.

Out into the World

Tolstoy arrived in St. Petersburg directly from the front line in fall 1855. He was greeted as a war hero and a promising new writer whom everyone wanted to meet and recruit for the different schools of thought about art and politics of the day. In the year and a half he lived in the capital, he participated more frequently in the life of the literary elites than ever before or again. Turgenev nicknamed him "troglodyte" for his uncouth army habits and his political incorrectness. He and others were astounded by the young officer's enormous physical and moral vitality and strove mightily to harness and direct it to what they considered good ends. Tolstoy himself was determined to maintain his independence and often baited friends like Turgenev for their, as he saw it, weak moral compass. But although he was a force ultimately beholden to no one, under the influence of cultural leaders of the day he indulged the passionate, artistic side of his complex nature and grew tremendously.

He read prodigiously, including works by William Shakespeare, Alexander Pushkin, Charles Dickens, Johann Wolfgang von Goethe, Miguel de Cervantes, and others. In literary polemics of the day, he sided with advocates of the sympathetic portrayal, which he associated with Pushkin and Dickens, over that of satire, associated with Gogol. He attended the theater, concerts, and operas. In 1857, he spent several months touring Europe, where, having witnessed a guillotining in Paris, he committed himself once and for all to a life of writing and reflection rather than public service. Under the influence of this seminal experience, he wrote a friend, "I will never serve *any* government anywhere." His diary entry that same day reads "A strong impression that will leave its mark. I am not a political man. Morality and art. [These] I know, love, and can do." After that experience, he escaped civilization for Rousseau's homeland, Switzerland, where he spent two idyllic months. He wrote in his diary during that time, "I am gasping from love, both physical and ideal.... I am taking a very great interest in myself. And I even love myself for the fact that there is so much love of others in me."

Tolstoy's attitude toward love in this decade was complicated. In the university and in the army, he enjoyed an active sex life and paid the price for it with bouts of venereal disease. When he arrived in St. Petersburg, he impressed his new friends with his lustiness, visiting brothels and keeping a mistress for a few months. Even at that time, however, he was vaguely uncomfortable about just plain sex, and he daydreamed about an ideal wife and family life based on mutual respect and duty. In a letter from January 12, 1852, to his Auntie Yorgolskaya, he fantasized about a wife who would be "une personne douce, bonne, aimante, elle a pour vous le même amour que pour moi" [someone sweet, good, loving; she would have the same love for you as she does for me]. In the spring of 1856, he concocted a romance with Valeriya Arsenyeva, a country neighbor whose legal guardian he was. This short courtship was mostly epistolary and certainly indebted to his reading of his beloved Rousseau. He may have been imagining himself as the older husband Wolmar in *Julie, or The New Heloise*. In May 1858, at Yasnaya Polyana, he began an affair with a married peasant named Aksinya Bazykina. It lasted until his marriage in 1862 and Aksinya bore him a son, Timofey, who, so far as we know, was his only illegitimate child. Timofey, whom contemporaries claim was the spitting image of his father, became a coachman on the estate. Tolstoy declared in his diary early in the affair that he was "in love as never before" with Aksinya, and in 1860 he wrote that "it's no longer the feelings of a stag, but those of a husband for a wife." Tolstoy's relations with Valeriya became the inspiration for his novella *Family Happiness*, and the affair with Aksinya yielded two unfinished stories (*Idyll* and *Tikhon and Malanya*) in 1860. Finally, in his diary entry of November 29, 1851, he recorded homoerotic feelings for various friends and especially for Dimitri Dyakov, a retired officer and neighbor, with whom he remained close until the latter's death in 1891. There is, however, no evidence that Tolstoy engaged in sex with Dyakov or other men. Perhaps influenced by his reading of Plato's *Symposium*, he prized his love for men as the kind of spiritual, erotic intimacy that did not require sexual relations. Such feelings may underlie the intense friendship between Nikolenka, the protagonist of the autobiographical trilogy (*Childhood*, *Boyhood*, and *Youth*), and his high-minded friend Nekhlyudov, who first appears in *Boyhood*. The friendship between Pierre and Andrey in *War and Peace*, unique in Tolstoy's oeuvre, has a similar purity. It is striking that, although both characters love the same woman (Natasha), they do not compete to win her.

All the different facets of love in his life appear in Tolstoy's representations of it in his fiction, and their relation to one another evolves over the years. While abroad, he wrote (or started) such stories as *Lucerne* (1857) and *Albert* (1858), which incorporated his new ideas about love, art, and morality, and introduced a metaphysical, transcendental level related to them into his fiction for the first time. Those stories were unsuccessful with the public, and Tolstoy himself was dissatisfied with them. In 1859, he withdrew from literary life in the capital and lived mostly at Yasnaya Polyana. For a time, he turned away from literature and toward education, which became a lifelong interest.

Pedagogy

Earlier, in 1849, Tolstoy had briefly run a school for peasant children on his estate. In 1859, he founded another school there. Traveling in Europe between 1860 and 1861, around the time of the emancipation of the serfs, he visited schools in various countries and was horrified by the authoritarian style and rote learning prevalent in French and especially German classrooms. This was true even when the schools practiced what was considered to be cutting edge, progressive methodology. In England, with the help of Matthew Arnold, he was able to observe classrooms and interact with students. He met the

German-Jewish writer Berthold Auerbach, whose novel, A *New Life* [*Neues Leben*], inspired his own anti-systematic pedagogy.

Back in Russia, he set up other schools in the Tula district in addition to the one on his estate. His ambition for these schools was grand. He hoped they would become a template for popular education in Russia, in which newly freed serfs would become literate and thoughtful without losing what he imagined to be their natural goodness. In this way, he would turn a minus—what others might perceive as Russian backwardness—into a plus by helping to develop a modern society without the distortions he had observed being inculcated in European classrooms. Tolstoy's attempts to promote literacy were controversial and viewed by government bureaucrats who paid attention to them as a potential threat to the State. In 1862, while he was away in Samara province, police raided the estate looking for forbidden materials brought there by the young teachers working in the school to distribute among the peasants. They found nothing. Tolstoy was so outraged by this intrusion that he considered emigration.

He founded a monthly newsletter entitled *Yasnaya Polyana*, in which he published various materials, including compositions by students, reports on classroom practice, and his articles on pedagogy. The articles called for maximum flexibility and freedom in the classroom, as well as equality among students and between students and teachers. Success in pedagogy, according to Tolstoy, depends upon the enthusiasm of the teacher for his subject, which then inspires the students. It is a form of infection just like art. As a Rousseauian utopian, Tolstoy believed that children and peasants are closer to moral perfection than adults, and that natural harmony in the soul was disrupted by civilization. In one of his most famous articles, "Who Learns to Write from Whom: Peasant Children from Us or We from Them?" he claimed to have learned more from the children than they did from him.

Tolstoy also wrote in this article about the difference between the "artistic" and the "unartistic" word: "[e]very artistic word, whether it belongs to Goethe or Fedka [one of Tolstoy's students], differs from an unartistic one in that it summons up a countless number of thoughts, images and explanations." This concept of the depth and breadth of each artistic word helps explain a peculiarity of Tolstoy's poetics, namely the role of repetition. Repeating a word several times in a sentence or a passage, he draws attention to its importance. Repeating it in many different passages, he invites his reader to contemplate its complex meaning. This, and not lectures or preaching, is the way to impart knowledge to students and to readers. Tolstoy made this point in "The Yasnaya Polyana School in November and December. Article One."

> You have to give the student opportunities to acquire new ideas and words from the general context of language. Once he has heard or read an unknown word in a sentence he understands, then another time in another sentence, he will begin to grasp the new idea vaguely, and he will finally feel, by chance, the necessity of using that word; he will use it once, and the word and the idea become his own.

Tolstoy provided examples of work written by his students, and insisted that their voices, not his, informed it. Students' voices mingled with his in a way that must have been exquisitely satisfying to him. He was very close to the boys he taught. In the article just quoted, he described a magical nighttime conversation with a group of them in which, he claimed, they said everything that could be said about "utility" and "physical and moral beauty." In his own mind at least, Tolstoy achieved a perfect friendship with his students akin to what he desired to have with his readers.

So art was very much on Tolstoy's mind even while he applied himself to pedagogy. He could not abandon literature for long, and he began to write again. In 1863, he published *The Cossacks*. It received a mixed reaction in the press, but close friends whose opinions he cared deeply about—for instance, his relative and lady-in-waiting, Aleksandra Andreyevna ("Alexandrine") Tolstaya, and the finest lyric poet of the time, Afanasy Afanasevich Fet—received it ecstatically. However much he praised the compositions of his peasant students, *The Cossacks* stands far above their writings in the way it conveys the author's complex vision through art.

The Cossacks

This work was the masterly culmination of the previous decade, as well as a gateway into the 1860s and Tolstoy's seminal novel, *War and Peace*. *The Cossacks*' first surviving antecedent is an 1853 poem called "Hey Mariana, Stop your Work!" in which the female protagonist joins other villagers in welcoming back their Cossack warriors and learns that her beloved has been killed. Part ballad and part ethnological sketch, this early poem reflects its young author's fascination with a place and people he identified with Rousseau's savage state of civilization. The finished work is a meditation on the culture of the mountain people and his outsider status in it. It is also a coming-of-age novel. The hero, Dmitri Olenin, returns to nature from civilization but discovers that he can't be a savage man like Cossacks Lukashka and Eroshka. Neither can he convince the beautiful Cossack maiden Marianka to marry him. Though she seems to toy with the idea, in the end, she chooses Lukashka over Olenin.

The work also explores the contradictions of love. Up until his journey, Olenin has been loved by others, but has never loved anyone except himself. He goes to the Caucasus in search of true love and a meaningful life. His last name means "stag" [*olen'*], and in a crucial experience on a hunt in the Caucasus, lying in the lair of a stag he has startled but does not succeed in shooting, he discovers a capacity within himself for self-sacrificing love. It is a strange moment, in which Christianity is associated with nature. In the grip of this kind of love, Olenin resolves to cede Marianka to Lukashka. Ultimately earthly love, also associated with nature, wins out over the Christian kind and Olenin moves aggressively to take Marianka for himself. He shifts from feelings of intense friendship for Lukashka to jealousy of him. Marianka does not cooperate, however. Unnoticed by Olenin, but apparent to an attentive reader, his courting of her is secondary to the love story between her and Lukashka. As an ideal couple of the younger generation in the village, they are attracted to each other and act out the dynamic between male and female at the base of Cossack life. He wants to bed her, but she turns him down, so as to force him into marriage. She wants him to commit himself to her, but he refuses in order to remain proudly aloof from a love that might unman him. In the end, he proves his loyalty to her by his courage in a sortie against enemy mountain men in which he is gravely wounded. His willingness to sacrifice for the commune seems to be the salient point for her. Meanwhile, Olenin, whether in the name of self-sacrificing or earthly love, acts only on his own behalf and in response to his own inner needs. In this respect, no matter what he chooses, he is more of an egotist than the savage men of the Caucasus. In this particular manifestation of friendship, Olenin's relationship with Lukashka may be as—or more—important to him than his love of Marianka because he wants so much to be like his Cossack friend.

A turning point in the long gestation of *The Cossack* occurred in the summer of 1857 when Tolstoy read Homer's *Iliad*. Homer became another foundational writer for him, one to whom he repeatedly returned throughout his life. Under the influence of the Greek master, he discarded the sentimental lens through which he had previously viewed Cossacks in his drafts. Most particularly, his youthful Cossack (the predecessor to Lukashka) no longer succumbed to romantic love for Marianka. The dominant ethos of the Cossacks became, as in Homer's world, expressed by the Russian word *sila*, meaning "force" or "strength." This sets up the plot between Lukashka and Marianka as outlined above, but also creates a tension between strength and love that interferes with a simplistic preference for nature over civilization. After all, the latter brought us Christianity and therefore can't be all bad. Yes, Olenin seems to discover Christian love in the stag's lair, but he does so through a process of reasoning that takes him out of unreflective nature. Both

Lukashka and the older Cossack Eroshka are aware of this danger to their strength. Lukashka, therefore, refuses to follow Olenin's train of thought about the morality of Lukashka's joy at killing an enemy warrior. Eroshka flies into a rage when Olenin asks him if as a young warrior he killed anyone; he prefers not to revisit the past in that regard.

The character of Olenin was criticized by some (including Turgenev) as an expression of Tolstoy's didacticism, but he represented Tolstoy's need to write everything he knew about human nature into his art. The self-conscious seeker Olenin is not a Lukashka, and he cannot be. So the work ends with the protagonist leaving the Cossack village to continue his life's journey with dreams unfulfilled. The departure scene is one of those concrete, realistic moments with deep, symbolic undertones frequent in Tolstoy's mature art.

The work that became *The Cossacks* was originally intended to be a fourth installment of *Four Stages of Development* (and therefore at one time was entitled *Young Manhood* in the drafts). It is significant that it, unlike the autobiographical trilogy, is in the third person. First-person narration, presenting a subject from his or her own point of view, is vital to Tolstoy's psychological realism, grounded as it is in subjective experience. Reality is always greater than one person's perspective on it, however. Even in *Childhood*, the narrator, shifting from the child's immediate experience to an older Nikolenka's recollections to an objective narrator's reflections on the text, actually represents more than one point of view. In *The Cossacks*, Tolstoy uses various narrative strategies—for instance, direct speech, indirect discourse, letters, and ethnographic commentary—to depict its central theme, which is the clash of two worlds.

The theme of love links *The Cossacks* with *Family Happiness* (1859). Both share with *Three Deaths* (1859) and *Polikushka* (1863) a bracing and, for some, too harsh realism. *Family Happiness* was Tolstoy's first attempt to unite romantic and prosaic love, and in it the intimacy and romance of courtship and early marriage give way to a partnership of parents. In *Three Deaths*, the demise of a tree appears more harmonious than that of a gentry woman or a peasant. All these works reflect the influence of Homeric realism on Tolstoy's art, and they too paved the way to *War and Peace*.

Marriage and the end of the long 1850s

In 1862, 34-year-old Tolstoy met and married 18-year-old Sofya Andreyevna Behrs, the daughter of a prominent Moscow physician. Her mother, a childhood friend of Tolstoy's, was only two years his senior and had been the model for Sonya in *Childhood*. The ardent lover proposed on September 14 and insisted (like Levin in *Anna Karenina*) that the wedding take place immediately. It was celebrated on September 23, and the newlyweds set out by closed carriage, without a honeymoon, for Yasnaya Polyana. City girl Sofya Andreyevna had agreed to forgo a trip to Europe, and she spent most of the next 19 years at the estate. Energetic and strong-willed, she was a remarkable person in her own right. She was musical, painted, and later in her life took up photography. She kept a diary and wrote stories. She took her role as the wife of a great man seriously, and from the very beginning of the marriage did everything she could to support him and his writings. The mother of 13 children of whom eight lived to adulthood, she gave Tolstoy the family and married life he had dreamed of, and which became the subject of many of his mature works.

2. *War and Peace* and the 1860s

War and Peace tells the story of several families and individuals during the period of the Napoleonic wars of the early 19th century. It begins in 1805. Old Prince Nikolay Bolkonsky and his daughter Princess Marya are living in the countryside at their Bald Hills estate, located near the city of Smolensk. A former general under Catherine the Great, he has taken up private pursuits like Marya's education while keeping a close eye on politics. In Moscow, the Rostov family is celebrating the name-day of the Countess and her enchanting 13-year-old daughter Natasha. (Name-days commemorate the saint after whom a person is named, and are not always the same as birthdays.) Natasha has a crush on Boris Drubetskoy, whose mother is a close friend of Madame Rostova. Natasha's brother Nikolay is looking forward to joining the army and is in love with his distant cousin, orphan Sonya, who lives with the family. Elsewhere in the city, old Count Bezukhov is dying and relatives scheme to inherit his fortune, which eventually goes to his bastard son Pierre. He and Andrey Bolkonsky (old Prince Bolkonsky's son and Marya's brother) are best friends, and we meet them first in St. Petersburg, where the dreamy Pierre has gone to consult Andrey on his choice of career. Handsome, well-connected, and rich, Andrey is already disillusioned with conventional success, including his wife Lise, beautiful but conventional, and pregnant with their first child. Lise dies in childbirth, and five years later Andrey starts courting Natasha. He proposes to her against his father's wishes, but while he is away in Europe attending to a war injury, she is seduced by and almost elopes with Prince Anatole Kuragin. (The Kuragins are a predatory St. Petersburg family that wreaks havoc in the novel.) Andrey cannot forgive her until he is on his deathbed after a second injury, incurred at the Battle of Borodino. Meanwhile, Pierre marries the sexy, loose Helene Kuragin. She eventually dies, probably from a botched abortion, and Pierre is free to marry Natasha, whom he has secretly loved since her engagement with Andrey. Old Prince Kuragin, who arranged the marriage between Pierre and Helene, fails to marry off Anatole to Princess Marya. Through a series of events probable only in wartime, Marya and Nikolay Rostov meet and court. He rescues her from capture by the French after her father's death, while she is coping with a possible peasant revolt. In a misstep fatal to her happiness, Sonya subsequently releases Nikolay from his promise to marry her. In the final episode of the novel, in 1815, the two happy couples—Marya and Nikolay, Pierre and Natasha—as well as their children, are together at Bald Hills, which Nikolay, retired from the Hussars, is now managing. Sonya and the old Countess live with the young Rostovs, as does Nikolenka, Andrey's orphan son.

Tolstoy wrote the novel during the happiest period of his life, and on a personal level, it is a paean to that happiness. The first mention of the work appears in a tender, joyful letter to his wife's sisters written a few days after his wedding: "[I'm] drawn now to free work *de longue haleine*—a novel or something like it." The French idiom *de longue haleine* means something like "hard work" both mental and physical, but its literal meaning is surely significant, too. In the middle of his life's journey, Tolstoy stopped, took a deep breath, looked backward rather than forward, and set out to write a capacious work that would celebrate life with its joys and suffering.

When Tolstoy married, he put aside his work on popular education. Instead, he turned from social concerns to story-telling, though this was not as much of a change as it might seem at first thought. In "The School at Yasnaya Polyana in November and December. Article one," he claimed that only hands-on experience could guide a teacher; according to him, unschooled or inexperienced people are not interested in history unless it is personalized and told through stories. One of the most memorable classes he ever taught was a lesson on Russia's war with Napoleon. This, he said, was not history, because "it was all in an almost fairy-tale tone, for the most part historically inaccurate, and centered around one historical personage [Napoleon]." He did not summarize his whole tale because he planned to publish it. He did not do this, and we can see his fairy-tale as one source of *War and Peace*.

Before their marriage, Tolstoy had shown Sofya his early diaries with their accounts of his womanizing, drinking, and gambling. (As a result, she was intensely jealous of his former lover Aksinya, who worked on the estate.) He wanted perfect intimacy with his future wife, even if it meant revealing all his faults, and at first, it seemed to him that he had achieved this. In 1864, in a letter to her from Moscow, where he was away from Sofya for three weeks while doctors tended to a broken arm he suffered while hunting, he wrote her that "like a good wife, you think of your husband as yourself." This was bliss for him and for her, too. On November 11, 1866, she wrote to him that "I love you so much, my sweet, and without you I am such an insignificant creature." Not that they were the same: as they understood it, she was more emotional, and he was more thoughtful. Even if this difference in characters could lead to petty conflicts, in a deeper way, they complemented each other. One possible sign of their closeness was the striking fact that between 1865 and 1878, there are almost no entries in Tolstoy's diary. He and Sofya were living together as soul mates, and he could confide his thoughts directly to her, rather than putting them down on paper. In the six years that it took him to write *War and Peace* (1862–1868), four children were born to them. As he wished, Sofya nursed their infants herself (except their last daughter Aleksandra, born in 1884 at a time when her parents were on very bad terms)—no wet nurses, as in Rousseau's *Emile, or On Education*—and she also nourished his art, copying and recopying thousands of pages as he obsessively rewrote his great epic. (She loved this activity, and continued it even after rocky times began in the 1880s.) The family mostly lived at Yasnaya Polyana, and Tolstoy left it only for brief periods; when he did so, he desperately missed his wife. On his property, he farmed and introduced many innovations, most of which were not successful. When he was not writing or managing his estate, he hunted. Family came and stayed for weeks at a time. He had settled his young wife in a wing without the grand features of the house that he had sold in the 1850s. He tried to devote part of each day to writing, though he found it difficult to do that in the summer. His study was tucked away from the bustle of a lively household in a first-floor room that had once been a storeroom; it had low arches, two windows, and hooks on the ceiling from which goods had been hung. It was in that room that Tolstoy wrote *War and Peace*, *Anna Karenina*, and many other works. While her husband wrote, Sofya was running the household. She supervised the domestic staff, planned three meals a day, and looked after the house. She had been trained as a teacher and, in consultation with her husband, oversaw the education of the children. In the gentry tradition, they were taught at home by a group of tutors and governors, but she herself occasionally prepared study materials for them. She also sewed clothes, and made blankets and various coverings that are displayed today at Yasnaya Polyana and in the Tolstoys' Moscow house, bought later. In the evenings and on breaks during the day Tolstoy participated as he wished in family activities. He joked, chatted, and played four-handed piano with his wife. In the mornings, he went on long walks or horseback rides either alone or with company. In short, from the time of Tolstoy's marriage, he was living the life described in the first epilogue of *War and Peace*. Like Nikolay Rostov, he farmed, while Sofya, like Natasha and Marya, looked after the children and the household. Exaggerating, one could even argue that the whole work exists to ground the family idyll that ends it. Yet there are hints in the final episode that the idyll cannot last. Pierre is not a writer, but a political activist, who quarrels with his conservative brother-in-law Nikolay. Young Nikolenka Bolkonsky, who listens to their conversation and takes Pierre's side, dreams of glory such as his father Andrey achieved. The book Tolstoy wrote is over, but he wants to make the point that life and history go on.

Historical Context

Outside the idyll, three historical events underlay the writing of the book. The first two were the Decembrist Uprising of 1825 and the Crimean War, 1853-56. The Uprising was a revolt led by the aristocracy in which, for the first time in the history of such occurrences in Russia, there was an attempt to change the political regime. Tsar Alexander I had died unexpectedly, far away from the capital and without a male heir. His youngest brother Nikolay eventually assumed the throne, but in the interregnum elite officers rebelled in the south and in the capital. The revolt was suppressed, the ringleaders were executed, and many participants were imprisoned and exiled. Almost every noble family in the country was affected, including Tolstoy's. His relative Prince Sergey Volkonsky was exiled to Siberia, and his glamorous young wife followed him there. Thirty years later, in 1856, after the death of Tsar Nicholas I, Decembrists were amnestied. Tolstoy met the Volkonskys in Florence in 1860, and soon after he conceived the idea of a novel called *The Decembrists*. Though he worked on it off and on for the next 20 years, and it was published in unfinished form in 1884, it also paved the way to *War and Peace*. (The male hero is named Pierre, and his wife—Natalya, or Natasha.) As Tolstoy himself explained the progression, he went from 1856 (when Pierre and Natalya return with their children from exile in Siberia for Pierre's participation in the revolt), back to 1825, and then to 1812 (as the event that arguably had planted seeds of political reform in the minds of officers who had conquered the invading French army, but while doing so were themselves infected by ideas of political liberty). Then, Tolstoy continued, for reasons of modesty he went back another few years, to recount the series of defeats that preceded Russia's greatest triumph. From 1812 on, the country was regarded as Europe's greatest military power. That status came to an end with its defeat in the Crimean War, fought against the British, the French, the Ottoman Empire, and Sardinia—a loss which so humiliated Tsar

Nicholas I that it may have contributed to his death. Without his own battle experience on the front lines in Sevastopol, Tolstoy could not have written *War and Peace*—note how often the artillery appears in the work—but one might also conclude that, having fought in a war that Russia lost, he conceived the idea of a work portraying a glorious victory.

As often happens when countries lose wars, recriminations, dissatisfaction, and calls for reform followed the Crimean War, eventually resulting in the emancipation of the serfs in 1861. This was a third underlying impetus to *War and Peace*. Welcome as it was, the emancipation did away with the old structure of the country without a clear blueprint for a new one. Among other things, *War and Peace* should be regarded as a representation of a moment of national unity that could inspire a newly disunified and potentially dispirited country. The first and most significant reform, the emancipation itself, required a new understanding of the Russian nation. In 1861, Tolstoy was among the 100,000 members of the gentry who owned 23 million serfs, almost 40 percent of the population. He took this societal role seriously, first planning a novel in 1852 depicting a good serf holder but then, in 1856, publishing a short story entitled *A Landowner's Morning*, in which the well-meaning protagonist is unable to help his serfs because the master-slave dynamic makes trust between the two impossible. The story is the first to express Tolstoy's obsession with freedom as the cornerstone of all social justice. Though he worried about the ruinous effects of emancipation on his own class, he favored it nevertheless, and he settled generous land claims on his peasants both before and after it. In 1861, he agreed to become Arbiter of the Peace to resolve disputes between peasants and their former masters. This was his only government job (aside from a brief and meaningless stint in the civil service in 1850), and, after running battles with recalcitrant neighboring landowners, he resigned from the post in disgust in 1862. Despite his dislike of politics, it is clear in *War and Peace* that he still took his responsibilities as a Russian nobleman seriously. To the extent that it had as one of its purposes the depiction of a Russian nation, the novel played a positive role in the creation of a modern Russian self-identity, and it continues to do so to the present day.

Writing a Historical Novel

War and Peace is the only historical novel published by Tolstoy. He worked on three others that he did not complete: The Decembrists, described above; an untitled novel set in the time of Peter the Great (1870-73, 1878-79); and Hadji Murat (1896-1904). For all three, he did a lot of historical research, and he insisted on their historical veracity, at least to a certain extent. In the case of War and Peace, he wrote that *"wherever in my novel historical figures speak and act, I have not invented, but have made use of the materials, from which, during my work, I have built a whole library, the titles of which I have found it unnecessary to set down here, but which I can cite if need be"* ("A Few Words Apropos of the Book War and Peace"; the emphasis is Tolstoy's). It is striking that he did not claim in this statement to provide a true account of events themselves. The reason for this, as it became clear in his arguments in the novel about history in digressions, and especially in the Second Epilogue, was that he did not believe that such an account was possible. What we have, from memoirs, letters, diaries, and various other documents, are voices of contemporaries from the epoch being studied, and accounts from them and others of their speeches and deeds. Historians build their works from such "materials," some of which, as Tolstoy argued in his essay, are more reliable than others.

He was especially dubious about official accounts of battles submitted by combatants. He also scoffed at the notion that official battle plans were ever actually implemented. In his opinion, expressed in various places and illustrated in his fiction, we can never know everything that happened in the past. Surviving historical materials do not add up by themselves to a complete or even coherent account of events. History, therefore, requires imagination to connect the speeches and deeds of historical figures as they come down to us. The poet is superior to the historian in this regard, and art is superior to history understood as a science. In addition to historical materials, in creating *War and Peace*, Tolstoy borrowed from artistic products—poetry and fiction—both from and after the Napoleonic war period. With all this in mind, as a poet, Tolstoy set out to provide an authoritative account of the epoch he described, and so far as its effect on subsequent history is concerned, he succeeded in accomplishing this. He called his approach "History-Art," and he said in a diary entry from April 5, 1870, that history practiced this way is the highest form of art. What he seemed to have meant by this was that "History-Art" records and analyzes the interaction of the human with inhuman forces partly created by people and partly by chance; and it can only do this by combining facts with imagination.

To help him imagine the past, Tolstoy needed a personal connection to it, and that was not hard for him. Writing *War and Peace* only a half-century after the events described in it occurred, he met and talked with many people who experienced these events first-hand. He was especially interested in their reactions to his novel. His own father had fought in the war, of course, and during his childhood Leo would have heard a lot about it from him and his war comrades. Living at Yasnaya Polyana with its archive of family letters and objects, talking about the past to extended family and friends (themselves often living in homes occupied by generations of the same family), reading published histories, memoirs, and diaries, helped Tolstoy construct an imagined past from all these elements.

Poetics

Of course, such an enormous body of work did not come from

nowhere. It is in the family of Russian historical novels influenced by Sir Walter Scott, chief among them Alexander Pushkin's novel *The Captain's Daughter* (1836). Eikhenbaum explained in *The Young Tolstoy* how the 1850s can be regarded as a training period during which the author constructed the parts—family and gentry life (*Childhood, Boyhood, Youth; A Landowner's Morning*), romantic love (*Family Happiness*), war (the Caucasian stories, the Sevastopol sketches, *The Cossacks*)—from which he then assembled the novel. In the same book, Eikhenbaum also showed how Tolstoy wanted to write long works from the beginning. Thus, as we have seen, *Childhood, Boyhood, Youth*, and *The Cossacks* are parts of the same project; *A Landowner's Morning* is the only publication resulting from *The Novel of a Russian Landowner*, and there are drafts of a continuation of *The Cossacks*. In this way, too, *War and Peace* may be regarded as the successful culmination of a trend present in the author's aesthetics from the beginning. Life is boundless, and the great realist Tolstoy wanted to capture that quality in his art.

Readers have been puzzled by the form of *War and Peace*. To achieve the impression of reality, it had to seem to be simple and clear—the highest aesthetic values for Tolstoy—but it is not. It is a unique, hybrid literary work with elements of historical chronicle, different types of novel, and epic. The first thing that strikes us about the opening of the work is its historical character. The protagonists talk about contemporary politics in such detail that readers need notes to follow what is going on. They speak in a language that Russian readers of Tolstoy's day would recognize as historically colored. They also dress in historically appropriate clothing. At the same time, this is a psychological novel. Therefore, although they may inherit certain traits from Tolstoy's family or even from himself, none of the characters or families mentioned above are strictly autobiographical. All conform to general rules of human nature and culture as Tolstoy understands and illustrates them. Furthermore, not once in the first part or anywhere else in the work does Tolstoy ever explain an action as due solely to the "times." Not one character simply represents the historical moment, as if it were fundamentally different from today. Thus, in that same historically colored opening, the motivations of the characters are all psychologically comprehensible. Anna Pavlovna has "la grippe" [flu] because it is trendy to do so. Later, in the same part, Julie Karagin writes to Princess Marya in the sentimental language of the day, and it is clear that this is an act of self-importance and self-definition. When Marya replies to her friend, however, her sentimental pietism is shown to be admirable. Here, as everywhere in Tolstoy, character is fate, and characters are embedded in history while not being ultimately defined by it. So, Anna Sherer and Prince Vasily Kuragin appear in that first scene as people of their times because they live by rules of *amour propre* [a form of self-love that requires the approval of others] that make them embrace convention over the movements of the heart. Later in the novel, we watch Boris Drubetskoy, who starts out in more authentic Moscow, move into the world of St. Petersburg for the same psychological reasons. As great historical events of the time take center stage, the reactions to them of various individuals—either fictional or historical ones—become keys to their character. Napoleon embraces the necessary role of commander of a great army because he loves glory and lacks compassion. Kutuzov takes on the same role to save Russia while limiting, to the extent possible, the death and the suffering of his own men and the enemy.

Though Tolstoy loved them, the closely-knit plots of English and French novels did not encompass his vision for the work. He could produce such plots: an example of one embedded in the novel would be the intrigue in the first part surrounding Count Bezukhov's will. In his Preface to *The Tragic Muse*, Henry James included *War and Peace* in the category of Victorian novels that he called "large loose baggy monsters." Contrary to James's opinion, however, there is nothing "loose" or "baggy" in the poetics of *War and Peace*. Tolstoy's narrator engages his reader through appeal to the senses and experience, and, when the narrator speaks in maxims, to reason. Instead of compelling his reader forward through plot, Tolstoy invites the reader to analyze his fictional world laterally, by means of comparison, which is used on a grand scale from the novel's beginning. Comparisons and epic similes recalling Homer and used to describe war and peace alike are present everywhere in the book. The title itself, of course, invites comparison. Volume 1, Part 1, takes place in three locations—St. Petersburg, Moscow, and Bald Hills, the country estate of the Bolkonskys. The truth in *War and Peace* is not to be found in any one of these locations: each one has both negative and positive qualities. This applies even to St. Petersburg, which seems like such a negative place at first glance. The underlying passion animating Anna Pavlovna's salon is an ugly one: vanity. But since vanity is one, though a low manifestation of pride, it is appropriate that Prince Andrey appears first in St. Petersburg. Once truly understood, pride leads to a hunger for virtue that cannot be all bad in Tolstoy's worldview. He realized this while writing *War and Peace*, and this is why, having first planned to kill off Andrey in the Battle of Austerlitz in 1805 as a cautionary tale against pride and love of glory, he resurrected him to live through many more pages and die heroically of wounds sustained at Borodino. St. Petersburg is also the proper place to ponder not only careers, but also true vocations. So in Part 1, Pierre talks with Andrey there about what he will do with his life. In Moscow, there are no such discussions. Bald Hills under old Prince Bolkonsky represents a life of virtue and reflection outside of history and society, but time stands still there. Characters move between St. Petersburg, Moscow, and Bald Hills, and respond to them in ways appropriate to their natures. They also grow, for better or for worse, as they do this. Pierre, as the broadest character in the book, is at home in all three. Volume 1, Part 2, introduces the war theme, inviting comparison to Volume 1, Part 1, in this respect. The opening chapters of Volume 1, Part 2, about the parade side of war, correspond to the description of St. Petersburg in Part 1, while war itself is like Moscow, where the lively Rostov party and the death of the old count happen simultaneously.

Here, as in all of Tolstoy's works, point of view is complex. Within the narrative, the reader must always consider not only what is being portrayed but, just as crucially, who is portraying it. We see events within the novel through the eyes of various characters or an omniscient narrator; the narrative imperceptibly modulates from one mode to another. At times, the narrator's voice openly analyzes, philosophizes, or moralizes. As in a Platonic dialogue, the readers are once again invited to compare narrative and commentary, and when we do so we are at our most reflective. Some readers, like Sir Isaiah Berlin in *The Hedgehog and the Fox: An Essay on Tolstoy's View of History* (1953), reject the author's commentary as not adequate to the details of his story-telling, while others see the two as complementary.

On January 3, 1863, Tolstoy wrote in his diary that "the epic mode is becoming the only natural one for me." Much later, he said to Maxim Gorky about the novel that "without false modesty, it is like the *Iliad*." *War and Peace* is an epic in which even details purely related to the particular historical period of the Napoleonic wars are intimately linked to portraiture through psychology and eternal laws. The wars themselves are said to obey mysterious laws, thereby elevating them to the status of myth. As depicted in the novel, there are two rhythms within the epic—that of nature and history (which is depicted in it as a naturally or divinely sanctioned rhythm); and that of each individual life. These rhythms define the structure of *War and Peace*, containing all else within them. Within historical space, war and peace alternate, first from peace to war, then to an unsteady and ultimately unsustainable peace after 1807, leading up to a crescendo of war with the invasion of Russia in 1812 and the eventual expulsion of the French, and finally ebbing back into peace. The stirrings of the Decembrist Uprising are present in the Epilogue's family idyll. The epic life of each individual is not cyclical but linear, from birth to death, but one generation replaces the next in epic sequence. The main characters—Natasha, Marya, Pierre, Andrey, and Nikolay—all undergo educations that are complete at the novel's end, where we see Nikolenka Bolkonsky's education just beginning.

War and Peace provides an account of Russian life that, whether it is actually true or not, has become the accepted and unifying standard of a formative epoch and, as such, a founding myth of modern Russia. War is essential to this myth, and it is the dominant theme in *War and Peace*. Taking advantage of the work's enormous length, Tolstoy developed this theme systematically throughout the book, never repeating himself and always adding to it in all its complexity. Different characters represent different military types and take us through various stages of the military experience. Horrible as it is, war has its charm. The Rostov brothers, Nikolay and Petya, are newly minted junior officers in love with it. Each of them feels the surging vitality that the nearness of danger brings. There is tremendous irony here: war's reality, described in *Sevastopol in December* as "blood, suffering, and death," is the source of life lived to the hilt in a way rarely felt elsewhere. Nikolay Rostov is wounded but lives to become an experienced warrior, while his younger brother Petya dies in his first engagement. The text describes Petya's innocent, poetic exhilaration before the battle, his reckless conduct in it, his death, and his mother's terrible grief. Nikolay outgrows the army and becomes a gentry landowner; we see how that happens. Captain Tushin represents the mentality and actions of a frontline officer. In Volume 1, Part 2, Chapter 20, we see him and his artillery battery tipping the scales of battle at Schöngraben, and then observe him taking pity on the wounded Nikolay Rostov in the aftermath. Having played his part, Tushin disappears from the book except for a brief appearance, now missing an arm, in the hospital where Nikolay visits Denisov at Tilsit (Volume 2, Part 2, Chapter 18). A career officer, Tushin is descended from Captain Maksim Maksimich, depicted by Mikhail Lermontov in *Hero of Our Times*, and then from the stoical Captain Khlopov in *The Raid*. Denisov, based on a real-life Napoleonic era cavalry officer and partisan whose memoirs and poetry Tolstoy read, is all action, but still has Tushin's humanity. As a partisan, he is paired with and contrasted to Dolokhov, a killer at home in war. The staff officers also represent different types: the fun-loving Nesvitsky, the light-weight joker

Zherkov, the cowardly and hypocritical unnamed staff officer at Schöngrabern, or the social climber Drubetskoy. Amongst the general officers, Bagration is a hardened professional warrior unafraid to sacrifice himself or others (including Rostov, whom he sends on a very dangerous mission at Austerlitz). Like Bagration, General Kutuzov understands his role to be primarily that of a motivator on the battlefield, but he is portrayed as both more humane than Bagration and a prophet of Russia's inevitable victory in 1812. After Austerlitz, a chastened Tsar Alexander withdraws from the battlefield to serve as a motivator at home. Napoleon does not learn this lesson even at Borodino, where chaos and fate overwhelm all his calculations. The great mass of conscripted peasant soldiers mostly makes cameo appearances to illustrate various aspects of military life. (Cossacks like Nikolay's orderly Lavrushka are a special, warlike exception.) When in his dream after Borodino in Volume 3, Part 3, Chapter 9, Pierre says that he wants to be like "them," he means he wants to throw off the individualist motivations of officers in war and take on what he perceives to be the fatalism and stoic courage of the peasant soldier. Platon Karataev epitomizes these qualities, but also shows the way to live morally within the limits imposed by war. The stoicism of the peasant needs to be mobilized by leadership, however, before it coalesces into a fighting force. It is significant in this regard that Pierre cannot take Platon's path in one crucial respect. At the end of the book, in the first epilogue, we see him meddling once again in history. Whatever Tolstoy may have thought of the advisability of Pierre's actions, they do not in any way undermine his nobility. On the contrary, Pierre would be much diminished if he did not show leadership by joining his St. Petersburg friends in political intrigues. On the battlefield, there is Prince Andrey, the glory-seeker whose speech before Austerlitz on this topic (Volume 1, Part 3, Chapter 12) is one of the most poignant moments in the book:

> I don't know what will happen then, I don't want to and I can't know. But if I want this, if I want glory, I want to be

known to people, I want to be loved by them, then it's not my fault that I want it, that I want only it, that I live only for it. Yes, only for it! I have never said this to anyone, but, My God, what am I to do if I love only glory, people loving me. Death, wounds, the loss of family, nothing terrifies me. And no matter how precious, how dear many people—my father, sister, wife—the people most precious to me are, no matter how terrible and unnatural it seems, I will give them all up in an instant for a moment of glory, for triumph over people, for the love of me by people I don't know and will not know [...] And all the same I love and treasure only this triumph over them all, I treasure this mysterious force and the glory that is hovering above me in this mist.

We see the lover of glory in this speech from the point of view of an insider (as opposed to Pierre's outside point of view). In the 1812 campaign, as Andrey continues to discover the realities of war and soldiering, he leaves his post as Kutuzov's adjutant to command a frontline regiment. While the regiment waits in reserve (Volume 3, Part 2, Chapter 37), his fatal wounding seems completely random and useless, and it is often treated that way. But in fact, Andrey gets the heroic death he deserves. His unwillingness in extremis to fling himself to the ground to escape a whirling shell is a sacrifice of himself for others. It is an act of leadership and bravery that plays a crucial role in inspiring that general stoic "spirit" that astonishes the enemy and keeps the Russians upright and still fighting long past the time when, it would seem, they should have capitulated. As Andrey looks at the shell and wavers in the presence of looming death, "he remembered that people were looking at him." When he calls to his adjutant that it is shameful to give into fear, he is speaking to himself as well. He fears shame and cowardice more than death. This is the warrior mentality expressed in Tolstoy's late epic *Hadji Murat*, when the hero tells his life's story to a Russian officer. In the case of *War and Peace*, with Russia's very existence at stake, warrior courage is manifested in a situation that ennobles it to the highest degree.

Andrey's act of courage is one of many examples of how a soldier at war makes himself part of a larger whole. In the 1805 campaign, we see Nikolay Rostov going from imagined jousting with his commanding officer over honor to feeling part of his squadron as he advances into combat for the first time (Volume 1, Part 2, Chapter 8). Recognition of chaos and danger motivates this embrace of the whole. He and other soldiers in similar situations step outside the threatened shelter of their individual selfhood into the big tent of their unit. They expand their sense of self to include others, who become brothers, fathers, and sons. This fact of wartime psychology is illustrated in Tushin's battery at Schöngraben and in the artillery battery that Pierre joins at Borodino (Volume 3, Part 2, Chapter 31). In the latter case, when the young officer commanding the unit is killed, the squadron dissolves. Rostov and his fellow soldiers feel this safety in numbers and the greater power it seems to confer when they shout for joy in parades. Pierre observes it in the form of a common energy at work before and during Borodino, as masses of soldiers and peasant helpers fight and win the battle. As the defensive walls of self-love seem to crumble, a platonic element of loving the other more than oneself comes into play. Nikolay's love of the Tsar reflects this dynamic, with Nikolay, the lover who would sacrifice himself for the beloved. Andrey, on the other hand, with his ceaseless quest for glory, wants others to love him. He wants to be the perfect beloved, the godlike figure that he actually becomes in death, as dreamt by his son Nikolenka.

War also pervades the seemingly peaceful life in the novel. The Kuragins wage war in society to achieve their selfish goals, as does Dolokhov, who, among other dastardly deeds, sleeps with Helene Bezukhov and rubs Pierre's nose in his wife's infidelity. (He and Pierre then fight a duel.) But it is not only villains who are warlike in peacetime. The great hunt scene on the Rostov estate of Otradnoe, and the evening at Uncle's with music and dancing that concludes it, are substitutes for war in peacetime. These events are peacetime outlets for the human vitality that *War and Peace* celebrates. Successful women in the novel are vivacious and, to this extent, warlike as well. At the Christmas celebrations at Otradnoe, Natasha, engaged to Andrey but with the wedding delayed, is filled with energy that she should be expending on love. Instead, she wanders restlessly through the house, ordering servants and family around. When she travels without her mother to Moscow, she continues overwrought and is ripe for the picking by Anatole. Even Princess Marya, for all her virtue and piety, summons the strength of will to land her man in the end. (When he tries to leave after a formal visit, she challenges him to explain himself, and they exchange gazes that express and seal their love.) At the end of the novel, Marya has to agree with Natasha that Sonya loses out because she lacks egoism (Epilogue, Part 1, Chapter 7).

It is the psychology of war that interests Tolstoy. Neither in *War and Peace* nor anywhere else in his war writing does he discuss the rational side of it except to discredit it. Training is never depicted, logistics always fail, and all strategizing is debunked. Tolstoy would only agree with Prussian General and military theorist Carl von Clausewitz (who makes a bit appearance in the work [Volume 3, Part 2, Chapter 25]) that war is politics by other means, in the sense that both are only power struggles. But as it is depicted in *War and Peace* at least, without war there would be no national unity among the different classes of society.

3. The 1870s and *Anna Karenina*

Anna Karenina is organized around the lives and fates of two individuals—the title character and landowner Konstantin Levin. Although the two meet only once in the course of the novel, their stories are thoroughly interwoven both in the plot and thematically. Anna's marriage dissolves after she starts an affair with the dashing Count Vronsky but, tormented by insecurities and suspicions about her lover's infidelities, she eventually commits suicide by throwing herself under a train. Levin, meanwhile, courts and marries Katerina (Kitty) Shcherbatsky, who was once in love with (but spurned by) Vronsky. She is also the younger sister of Dolly Oblonsky, who is married to Anna's brother, Stiva. The numerous other characters and subplots are all related to these two lines in one way or another.

Background

The work is contemporary rather than historical, and in that sense provides a snapshot of a particular period that Tolstoy knew well. He could not structure his modern-day chronicle around an analysis of history and a historical period, the way he does in digressions and essays in *War and Peace*. Not only does *Anna Karenina* mostly take place at the time of writing (the 1870s), but Tolstoy also incorporated an event, the Russo-Turkish war (1877-78), that only began after the novel was well underway and parts of it had already been serialized in the periodical *The Russian Messenger*. As in *War and Peace*, characters react to this and to other historical circumstances in ways that reveal their own natures.

In the 1860s and 70s, Tolstoy was deeply involved in the education of his own children, which, in conformity with his wife's wishes, was more conventional than he recommended in his articles on pedagogy. The house was full of tutors hired to teach various subjects, and Tolstoy himself taught math. As he was finishing *War and Peace*, his interest in popular education re-emerged. In 1868, the first mention of a primer, or ABC book, occurred in his diary. In a letter of 1872 to his relative and close friend, Alexandrine, he wrote that "my proud hopes for the primer are these: that two generations of *all* Russian children, from those of the Tsar to those of the peasants, will learn using only this primer, and they will get their first poetic impressions from it, and that, having written this primer, it will be possible for me to die peacefully." In connection with this project, he re-established the school at Yasnaya Polyana, and his wife and two older children taught in it. He served on several education committees in the district, and, though he did not revive his formal journal on the subject, he wrote and published articles about pedagogy. One especially, "On Popular Education," generated a lot of discussion. He even gave a speech to the Committee for Literacy in Moscow in 1874. Tolstoy was now immensely famous as the author of *War and Peace*, and his pedagogical views received more attention than in the 1860s.

After an unsuccessful primer published in 1872, a much revised New Primer was published in 1875. Among other changes, it had dropped the section on arithmetic and was shorter and much cheaper. It was accompanied by four readers which contained many stories from the first primer as well as new ones. Recommended by the Ministry of People's Enlightenment, it was already into its second printing by December, and went through 28 editions in Tolstoy's lifetime. The primer and readers filled a gap Tolstoy had identified during the 1860s in his promotion of literacy. Without this textbook, there was nothing for his students to read that would help them transition from popular spoken language to the language of high culture, science, and politics. In classes at Yasnaya Polyana, they had floundered in *Robinson Crusoe* (a favorite among educated

Russians at the time) and had found Pushkin and Gogol, the greatest masters of Russian literature, boring and incomprehensible. When Tolstoy read to them from his beloved translation of the *Iliad* by Nikolay Gnedich, they thought it was in French. There was nothing in the published literature that described life as the students actually experienced it. By the early 1870s, when Tolstoy was working intensively on the primer, he had decided to learn the language of the people and write in it. His oldest son Sergey recalled how his father studied Russian oral traditions. He read texts known to the people already—the Bible, lives of saints, chronicles, and short Russian epic poems called *byliny*—and marveled at their beautiful, pure Russian. He also talked to locals as they went about their business, and he haunted the highway to Kiev that went past Yasnaya Polyana, conversing with pilgrims and other travelers. He borrowed from and rewrote some of their stories for his readers. At the same time, in 1870 he had taught himself Greek, and was now reading Plato, Homer, Xenophon, and others in their native language. Reading Homer in the original was like "seeing to the bottom of an ice-cold rushing stream." He declared that everything he prepared for the primer had to be in a language that was, in his words, "beautiful, concise, simple, and, most importantly, clear"; otherwise his peasant students would not learn from it. So Tolstoy rewrote, all in the same simple style, materials from many sources and on many subjects. Some works included in the 1875 primer and all of those in the readers had both a name and a designated category in their titles. The categories include fables, illustrations of folk sayings, poems, fairy-tales, fiction, stories taken from real life and Russian and world history, stories from his own life (including the one of a hunt in which he was almost killed by a bear, and six captivating stories about Bulka, the dog who went with him to the Caucasus), descriptions of exotic places, as well as accounts and scientific explanations of natural phenomena and creatures known to all. Most of the works were very short, with some longer ones interspersed. Though intended for children and adult peasant learners, some rise to the level of great art.

Another Great Novel

At the same time as he was absorbed in the reform of popular education, Tolstoy was thinking about a new novel, which turned out to be *Anna Karenina*. Both plot lines had deep personal resonance for the author. This is especially clear in the case of Levin, whose surname echoes Tolstoy's first name (Lev in Russian). By the time he began the work, he had been married for over 10 years and had five children. Although their relationship was tumultuous from the beginning, he and Sofya were very happy for 20 years, until a midlife crisis and religious conversion took him in a direction that she could not follow. It is during the second decade of this first period that he wrote *Anna Karenina*, which therefore benefits from his direct knowledge of marriage and family life. He borrowed from his own experience to tell the story of Levin's courtship, wedding, and first year of marriage. Another and related personal factor—an increased consciousness of the inevitability of death—was troubling Tolstoy at the time. His toddler son Pyotr died of croup in 1873, "the first death in our family in 11 years," as Tolstoy reported to his friend, the poet Fet; other deaths of young and old—two infants, "Auntie" Yorgolskaya, and Aunt Countess Pelageya—followed later in the decade. A renewed preoccupation with mortality threatened to undermine life for Tolstoy, who wove his anxiety into his novel. It precipitates Levin's crisis of faith after the death of his brother Nikolay, named after Tolstoy's own beloved older brother, who had died in his presence in 1860. (Tolstoy signals the importance of this event by calling the chapter [Part 5, Chapter 20] in which it occurs "Death." It is the only named chapter in the novel.) Levin's temptation to commit suicide, mentioned in Part 8, is also a detail taken from Tolstoy's life. At the same time, during this decade Tolstoy still occupied himself with his duties as a landowner, father, and family man. Like Levin, he tried to modernize farming practices on his estate. Tolstoy's attempts, like Levin's, mostly failed, though not, it seems, because he misunderstood or mishandled his peasant laborers as Levin did. His own farming failures seem to have been due to ineptitude or perhaps, to be more generous, impracticality; here again, he used but distorted his biography to make a point. In 1871, he built a large addition to the house at Yasnaya Polyana to accommodate his growing family. This experience is reflected in Levin's oversight of a building project in Part 6 of the novel. The same year, Tolstoy bought land to the east, in Samara Province, and he continued to travel there and to add to his holdings through the decade. He also began to breed horses that he grazed on his Samara pastures. He had been there in the 1860s to drink kumis, a fermented mare's milk that was considered very healthy. After two of his brothers, Dmitri in 1856 and especially Nikolay in 1860, had died of tuberculosis, he had worried that he, too, might be susceptible to this disease. Tolstoy also suffered from stomach problems, and kumis was supposed to be good for digestion. When he felt depressed and ill in 1871, Sofya urged him to travel again to Samara for his health. The Bashkirs who made kumis were a Turkic tribe indigenous to the region and, like the Cossacks, they lived a Homeric life that appealed to Tolstoy. In a letter he wrote to Fet from the province in 1871, he noted that he was reading works by the ancient Greek historian Herodotus, and he regretted having written such a long-winded book as *War and Peace*. (Here is yet more proof that the style of his stories for the primer and readers and his later emphasis on brevity in his prose owed something to the Greeks.) Once he owned land in Samara Province, he spent some summers there with the family, and twice (in 1875 and 1878) held races and games there for the local Bashkirs. Levin does not buy land in *Anna Karenina*, but Anna's brother Stiva Oblonsky sells a forest from his wife Dolly's property to a rapacious merchant, and Levin disapproves of this act because it is a violation of his duty as a gentryman to preserve and cultivate the land.

The connection of Anna to Tolstoy is more hidden, but also significant. If, as is often said, Levin is Tolstoy without the genius, who figures out how to compromise to live an orderly life, Anna (like

Prince Andrey in *War and Peace*) represents the romantic genius who dies in search of absolutes.

Like Tolstoy, the times in which he wrote this second novel had changed, too. The abolition of serfdom in 1861 had led to social, political, and legal reforms whose long-term consequences were still developing in the 1870s. The decline of the gentry class, the necessity of agricultural reforms to improve the status of newly freed and displaced peasants, the rise of a newly emboldened mercantile class and upstart parvenus, the organization of a more consultative political system: all these issues are vetted in the novel by Levin, who models the response to them of a decent gentryman. Underlying such changes and moving steadily forward was a modernization that featured industrialization, the increased secularization of society, the concomitant prestige of science, and the breakdown of traditional ways of life. In his young manhood, unself-consciously following current intellectual trends, Levin had embraced both secularization and science. He now finds himself without the moral foundation he needs to ground his sense of self-worth. It is this lack of higher meaning supporting the subjective self that he shares with Anna at the end of her life.

The work grew out of an idea Tolstoy mentioned to Sofya in 1870, about a fallen woman who was pitiful but not guilty. So the novel began with a character. As Tolstoy explained, other characters then grouped themselves around Anna to create the action. This process is typical of his mature art, and, paradoxically, one reason for his success as a philosophical novelist. His successful works of art are not treatises. First, characters came to him, then he thought about them. He could not make them act out of character to prove a point.

It is noteworthy, however, that one impetus to the novel was an experience Tolstoy had in 1872: he viewed the dead body of the mistress of a neighboring landowner who had thrown herself under a train. Anna was created to die by suicide, and this death is connected to the genre of the work. Its full title—*Anna Karenina. A Novel in 8 Parts*—signals that it is a novel, but one passage (Part 1, Chapter 20) relates the "novel" ("roman" in French) specifically to

Anna and her love life, or romance. The "novel" within the novel ends with Anna's suicide in Part 7. Life continues in her absence in Part 8, where Levin escapes despair and death because, without noticing it, he has grounded himself over time in the epic world of family and work. There he realizes that having "put his plow into the earth," he has left a furrow of good deeds that define his life and give it meaning. By contrast, from the time Anna abandons her husband Alexey and son Sergey for her passionate love affair with Count Vronsky (whose first name is also Alexey), she struggles unsuccessfully to find a meaningful new life. The theme of good, natural work, which expands to include helping one's family and neighbors but not to politics or business, links *Anna Karenina* to the *Novel of a Russian Landowner* of the 1850s. It is worth noting, however, that the epic world inhabited by Levin escapes tidy plotting. Even in the idyllic time that ends the novel he struggles and future crises loom in his life. Characters in *Anna Karenina* repeatedly struggle to "shape things up" (as Stiva's servant Matvey puts it in the opening scene). But that doesn't happen. In the middle of the novel (Part 4, Chapter 17), Anna almost dies giving birth to a daughter by Vronsky. She summons her husband to her bedside, where he forgives her. It seems that a repentant Anna will die, or the two will get back together and things will "shape up" into a neat ending. Instead, when Anna recovers, she returns to her affair with Vronsky, and her husband, after his astonishing moment of forgiveness, returns to his petty, vindictive self. Once Anna's romance with Vronsky cools, as it must, she has nowhere to go. Like Levin, she cannot live without meaning and, like him, she seeks personal happiness. She is not lucky, the way Kitty or Natasha (in *War and Peace*) are, to find a man worthy of her. (Neither her husband nor her lover turn out to be so.) She is not like Kitty's friend Varenka, who can live for virtue alone. Anna will not settle, the way Stiva's wife Dolly does, for less than perfect happiness. In her quest for true love, she even abandons her son. Ultimately, only Vronsky's continuing complete obsession with her can satisfy Anna, and without that, she descends into nihilistic rage and hopelessness.

The work is woven from all the different threads that underlie the speech and actions of characters. These include their social positions, their individual characters with all the conflicting or harmonizing facets, and the particularities of any situation in which they find themselves. One general organizing principle of the novel is the theme of family; there is hardly an episode or a character not connected to it. Later, Tolstoy said that in *War and Peace* he had been captivated by the idea of a people [*narod*], while *Anna Karenina* was about the family. The two "ideas" are related as ways to organize individuals into societies. Family in Tolstoy's opinion was part nature and part convention, and therefore able to bridge the gap between the two. Marriage allows us to experience romantic love and intimacy; once these feelings become enslaving, we can escape them and have a partnership focused on raising a family, which has its own satisfactions. (Children provide a sense of fulfillment; the desire to procreate is another response to our mortality.) The Levin marriage ceremony is depicted as a sacred event outside of time. At it, even Dolly, with all her disappointments, remembers Stiva in love on their wedding day, and she is reminded why she still wants to stay with her philandering spouse. Marriage is the bedrock of human society, the place in which children, future generations, can be nourished and educated, and where Tolstoy—as the student of Rousseau—hoped that duty and happiness could be reconciled. He saw the family as the place where we learn moral lessons for our entire life. So, for instance, Kitty is saved by her "upbringing," while such characters as Anna, Stiva, and Vronsky are partly led astray by bad or no upbringing. The family ideally shelters children from the chaos of the human passions. As Elizabeth Stenbock-Fermor points out (in *The Architecture of Anna Karenina: A History of its Structure, Writing, and Message*) the work begins with a dysfunctional family (the Oblonskys) and ends with a functional one (the Levins). Stiva's daughter Tanya must blush at the prevarications of her father. At the end of the novel, when baby Mitya Levin smiles at his family and frowns at strangers, he takes an enormous step from the natural animal egotism expressed in his first cry to more human sociability.

There is no single perfect family in the novel, however. In the struggle of circumstances and various impulses, the moral self often loses out, and this losing battle is repeatedly documented in Tolstoy's psychological prose. This fact of life creates the conditions for narrative rather than moral treatises. Appropriately, *Anna Karenina* begins with a famous maxim: "All happy families are alike; each unhappy family is unhappy in its own way."

Tolstoy meant to convey by this that happy families resemble each other because they abide by universal moral rules. Unhappy or imperfect ones, on the other hand, are all different, because, as the novel demonstrates first in comic (the Oblonsky family) and then in tragic (Anna and Vronsky) mode, people make poor choices. All the characters own their stories because, by choosing one element of the chaos around and inside them over another, they create these circumstances.

In real life, marriage turns out to be a compromise that cannot always satisfy our deepest longings for intimacy, and in Anna's story Tolstoy shows what happens when people sacrifice everything in a quest for perfection in this regard. Baby Mitya and Kitty enjoy an intimacy so intense, at least on the level of the body, that her milk comes before she hears Mitya's hungry cries. Kitty also imagines Mitya's nascent spiritual life, which will develop under her guiding love. This degree of closeness between mother and child does not survive infancy, however, and beyond courtship, neither the young Levins nor the old Shcherbatskys share such intimacy with each other in their successful marriages. In the novel, the craving for intimacy, whether it be that of Anna and Vronsky or Kitty and Levin, is one large justification for romantic love. It is natural, and therefore it cannot be simply denied. Tolstoy depicted its power, including the scene between Anna and Levin where, as Kitty correctly concludes in a jealous outburst when he returns home, she seduces him in mind if not in fact. Romantic love poses a serious threat to marriage and the novel, far from debunking it, demonstrates why this is so. In later works (*Kreutzer's Sonata, Master and Man, Resurrection*), Tolstoy soured on marriage and the family, while in *Anna Karenina* he still believed in them, and wanted to argue that life outside the family was incomplete.

Human Nature and Moral Agency according to Tolstoy

At one point in its creation, the maxim about happy and unhappy families was the novel's epigraph. Then it migrated to its first paragraph, and another epigraph–"Vengeance is mine; I will repay"–took its place. In 1907, Tolstoy told his son-in-law Mikhail Sukhotin that he had chosen the epigraph "to express the idea that the bad that one does has as its consequence everything bitter that comes, not from people but from God, and that Anna Karenina experienced." The epigraph, a variant of Deuteronomy 32:35, comments on the novel with Biblical weightiness, and no reader can deny that things end badly for Anna. But other characters–Stiva, Betsy Tverskaya, the merchant Riabinin–behave badly and do not suffer ill consequences. Children–Seryozha Karenin, and, in the future, the offspring of Stiva and Dolly–are innocent victims of the bad actions of their parents. For that matter, Vronsky may be the innocent victim of his mother's loose living when he was a child.

Nonetheless, in his interpretation of the epigraph, Tolstoy made Anna responsible for her fate. He believed in moral autonomy, and this is why he stressed it in his explanation to his son-in-law. I would argue this is the unifying factor of *Anna Karenina*, and I digress here to explain why. In the opinion of some critics, Tolstoy's characters are only fluctuating states of mind responding to inner and external stimuli. These critics point to the author's own assertion about human nature in a famous passage in his third and last novel, *Resurrection*.

> One of the most common and widespread superstitions is that every person has their own fixed qualities, that a person is good, evil, smart, stupid, energetic, lazy, and so on. People are not like that. We can say of a person that he is more often good than evil, more often smart than stupid, more often energetic than lazy, and the other way around; but it would not be true if we said of one person that he is good or smart, and of another, that he is evil or stupid. But we are always dividing up people this way. And this is untrue. People are like rivers. The water in all of them is the same, but every river is now narrow, now swift, now wide, now quiet, now clear, now cold, now murky, now warm. People are like that. Every person carries the beginnings of all human characteristics and manifests now some of these, now others and is often completely unlike himself, while remaining one and the same self. (Part 1, Chapter 59)

The principle embodied here is primary both in Tolstoy's fiction and in life (and history) as he understood it. Like nature, human life is governed by laws, both physical, and, in the case of human beings, psychological. Without such laws, there could be no science, philosophy, art, or even mutual understanding. Influenced both directly and indirectly by Rousseau (through such authors as Laurence Sterne), Tolstoy believed that the soul is constructed of elements related to the body and is influenced by reason, which distinguishes human beings from the animal in us. Human feelings range from animal instincts like the need to eat or have sex to passions like pride or a desire for virtue that employ our reason to compare ourselves to others or to meet inner standards. These standards may be set by convention, but they may also, as Levin learns in Part 8 of the novel, require us to listen to an "infallible judge" who resides in the soul. This judge is conscience, the voice of God, or, as Tolstoy once put it ("Religion and Morality," 1893), "infinite reason."

At the same time, chance—that is, the interaction of various internal and external circumstances—not only influences the individual and society, but also is a fundamental condition of human existence. Those who believe that they can control life's chaos—Napoleon in *War and Peace*, or Anna's husband in *Anna Karenina*—learn otherwise. Human agency, as Tolstoy understood it, does not extend beyond individual freedom for a very simple reason: if it did, it would diminish the freedom of others. Without such freedom, there can be no dignity and no self for which we take responsibility. This freedom makes it impossible for us to predict the future for ourselves or others. The human need for dignity and the freedom required for it trumps all else in Tolstoyan psychology and any social policy that does not take it into account is doomed to fail. This is why Anna's husband cannot create a workable "racial minorities" policy that does not consult the people affected, and Levin cannot create agricultural reform without taking into consideration the will of the worker-peasants.

Characters in the novel can't control themselves, and, as individuals, they are products of chance, too. Yet despite constant interaction among laws of human nature, chance, and necessity, moral choice exists within individuals in most, though not all, circumstances, and this potential for moral freedom generates, in Tolstoy' understanding, individual dignity. Levin, like the Oblonsky siblings, is an orphan, yet he turns out differently from them. He lives his life by heeding the voice of conscience, while Stiva and Anna at crucial moments ignore it. Dolly, like Anna, is dealt a poor hand in marriage, and yet she does not commit suicide or even leave her husband, though she is tempted to do so. Anna herself repents at the last moment her decision to throw herself under the train. This remorse comes too late to save her, but she is exercising free choice even in these extreme circumstances.

No writer of fiction has more thoroughly illustrated the interplay between circumstance and free choice than Tolstoy. Mixed into circumstances is a dominant principle of free will and moral autonomy in human nature that makes us responsible for our own fates, at least to some extent. Furthermore, those who acknowledge such responsibility are higher in the human moral universe than those who do not. Anna (unlike her brother Stiva) does feel responsible, at least most of the time. That fact makes Anna a tragic heroine rather than merely a victim, and justifies her status as the title character in the novel.

4. A Midlife Crisis

Tolstoy's life was shaped by a contrast and connection between life and death, joy and sorrow. His art is also a product of this dynamic. While he wrote some of the most joyful affirmations of life in modern fiction, he experienced dark moments in his personal life that arguably gave rise to those paeans in his prose. His first published work is about the death of the protagonist's mother: the author both recreates and reminisces about a precious intimacy that he has lost. Nikolay Tolstoy died of consumption in September of 1860, and Leo confided in his diary a month later that his death "has been the strongest impression of my life." After his brother's passing, life seemed meaningless to Tolstoy, and without meaning, he could not write.

> Again the question: Why? It's not long before I go there. Where? Nowhere. I'm trying to write, I'm forcing myself, and it's not working only because I can't ascribe to my work that meaning that I must have to have the strength and patience to work.

But Tolstoy's fear that he would not be able to continue writing turned out to be groundless. On the contrary, as if in defiance of his own and his brother's mortality, he began to churn out pages of *The Decembrists*, several peasant stories, and *The Cossacks*. He married and wrote *War and Peace*. Seen in this context, his characterization of this epic masterpiece as "a work *de longue haleine*" defines it as a breath of life, a rebellion by the poet against death and annihilation. In it, Prince Andrey, the character for whom life must make sense, or it will wither, dies so that less reason-minded figures like Natasha Rostova and Pierre can come together and flourish.

But even at the high point of Tolstoy's life—represented by *War and Peace*—trouble lurked. Before he finished the work, he had become captivated by the writings of the pessimistic 19th-century

German philosopher Arthur Schopenhauer, and especially by his idea that life is a dream, and death is reality. Andrey's death, in which he turns toward a mysterious truth that informs everything but is inaccessible to the living, already reflects Schopenhauer's influence. So does Nikolay Rostov's worry in the Epilogue that his wife and Andrey's sister Marya is too good to remain alive. Ominously, this moment in the novel is another reminder of the death of Tolstoy's mother. After *War and Peace*, the dynamic between the two poles of life and death in Tolstoy's life and his art began to shift. In 1869, while staying in the town of Arzamas during a business trip, he experienced an attack of what Russians call *toska*, a word with broad meaning that, borrowing from Vladimir Nabokov's long definition, might be translated as spiritual anguish. Then, in 1871, he suffered a serious bout of depression which felt to him like a step away from idyllic family life back to the loneliness that had afflicted him before marriage. It is significant that he wrote *Anna Karenina*, with its celebration of courtship and young married love, after the depression of 1871, when the happiest period of his marriage was in the past. As author and narrator, Tolstoy was now able to distance himself from that blissful time and depict it as a response to the ongoing *toska* inflicted by life. In this key respect, there is no difference between the needs of Levin and Anna. They yearn for intimacy and meaning, achieve both momentarily, and then lose them when that happy state slips away into something else. While the Dionysian love of Anna and Vronsky leads to her death and his death wish as he embarks for the front in the Russo-Turkish War in Part 8, the obsession of each with the other is not different from Levin's mad love for Kitty, without which the Levins' marriage would be virtuous but as unsatisfactory as that of the Karenins. At the end of the novel, in Part 8, Levin is resigned to a certain distance between him and Kitty, but they are united in the common task of raising and supporting a family.

Sofya, who noted the rift between her and Leo in her diary in 1871, attributed it to illnesses both had suffered that winter. Tolstoy was at the peak of his powers as an author, but in 1877, as he struggled to complete *Anna Karenina*, he complained again of depression and ill health. He began to attend church and observe fasts and other rituals to the point where his wife, for whom Russian Orthodoxy was a normal part of life, grumbled that he had become too religious. He consulted religious authorities and was dissatisfied with their teachings. By 1879, Sofya noted disapprovingly that he was moving away from the official church. He had decided that, seek though he might, he would not find a new life in it. As his trust in Orthodoxy declined, his interest in Russian sectarians grew. This was part of his political radicalization because there was no separation of Church and State in Russia, and deviation from official Church dogma was regarded as heresy. Once he turned from the Church, just as he did from the government and society, there was no hesitancy.

"Church and State" (1879)

A short essay written early in Tolstoy's quest for religious certainty and not published until much later already attacks the established Church in sharp, precise, and polemical tones. He claimed that the very idea of a church was anathema to Christianity in its original form, and arose from a conspiracy to force everyone to believe the same thing. In truth, he argued, each person is responsible for his own beliefs, and no one has the right to force these on others. Christianity became perverted when it aligned itself with power, specifically with Emperor Constantine. Before that, Tolstoy posited, the word subsequently translated as "church" meant simply an assembly of like-minded people. Charlemagne and Vladimir (the Kievan Russian prince who converted to Christianity in 988) followed the same path as Constantine, making Christianity pagan by absorbing subversive political principles into it. Hence, Tolstoy wrote, "the sanctification of state power by Christianity is blasphemy; it is the ruin of Christianity." The authority of the priesthood in all state-sanctioned Christianity depends on its original teaching of "humility, self-sacrifice, love, poverty; but the teaching is preached by force and evil." Tolstoy is distinguishing here between the theological dogmatism that had caused so many battles and crimes in history, and the moral, positive teaching of Christianity, agreed upon by all. Today, according to him, unadulterated Christianity remained in force only among religious dissenters.

****

In the 1880s, Tolstoy also turned decisively against the idea of government, and there were political as well as personal reasons for him to do so. *War and Peace* had been written against the backdrop of the so-called Great Reforms instituted by Tsar Alexander II and starting with Emancipation. Even although Alexander II turned conservative, he continued to roll out reforms throughout the 1870s, and, correspondingly, *Anna Karenina* reflects engagement in contemporary Russian politics. In Part 6, for instance, Levin attends elections for a local assembly as part of the so-called *zemstvo* system of official consultation by the autocrat with various classes.

Levin disapproves of most of what is happening there, but he participates, and, most importantly, elsewhere he expresses opinions about where he thinks the country should be going. (In the 1870s, Tolstoy himself participated in *zemstvo* activities related to pedagogy in Tula.) In 1881, Alexander II was assassinated, his son Alexander III ascended the throne, and a period of political repression set in that lasted until 1917. Having established some institutions of local self-government through the *zemstvo* system, the Romanov tsars still insisted upon retaining ultimate power. Even though certain reforms, mainly economic ones, continued to go forward, every effort was made to roll back political liberalization. A form of martial law originally imposed for three years after the assassination remained in place until 1917. Political rights, especially those of peasants, were curtailed, while the gentry, though in economic decline, was favored over other classes. Education was monitored, and to the extent possible, controlled. Russian nationalism grew and was encouraged by the authorities. Minorities like the Ukrainians and the Finns were persecuted, and there was religious oppression, supported by the Russian Orthodox Church—not only of non-Christians, but of Catholics, Lutherans, and Russian sectarians—as well. Pogroms broke out against the Jews, and the authorities did little to stop these. This was the government under which Tolstoy now lived, and when we read his condemnations of all government from the 1880s onward, we must keep this political context in mind.

Marital woes

The crisis between Tolstoy and his wife erupted into the open at the beginning of the decade. It's not that they ceased to love one another at this time or later—four children were born in the period from 1879-88—but as Sofya complained in letters to him, he was taking a new path along which she could not follow him. Chief among the personal causes for the crisis were aging and Tolstoy's feeling that he could no longer ignore his own looming death. He grew depressed again. The joy of life that animated all around him, and that expressed itself in his love of hunting, music, and family fun broke out less often. Also, he and Sofya parted ways on politics. The assassination of the Tsar led to bitter debates at Yasnaya Polyana, and Sofya was appalled when Tolstoy wrote to Tsar Alexander III requesting that his father's assassins be spared. (They were hanged on April 6, 1881.) He did not approve of the assassination, but he called—at the time and for the rest of his life—for evil to be answered not with revenge, but with Christian mercy. This, he thought, was the appropriate stance of the Russian autocrat. He took the executions personally, later comparing the agony of Sofya Perovskaya, one of the organizers of the assassination, to his own near-death by a bear on a hunting expedition in December 1858. (He describes the incident in 1875 in a short story for one of his readers called, in English, "The Bear-Hunt," and the skin of the slain bear is under the piano on the second floor of his Moscow home described below.) So this is yet another case of how the fear of dying shaped his life. In 1882, when he was elected to a three-year term as Marshal of the Nobility in Tula district, he declined to serve.

Sofya hoped that her husband's obsession with religion would pass, and their earlier, happier life would resume, but this did not happen. Officials began to spy on Tolstoy in 1882 because of his contacts in Samara Province with peasant sectarians—Molokans, Sabbatarians, and others—who rejected the teaching of the established Russian Orthodox Church. Even more disruptive for family harmony, he began to call for a radical simplification of their lives. He lost interest in farming and horse-breeding. He also proposed that the family give away much of their property, wean themselves from servants, live in a few rooms (one bedroom for the boys and one for the girls), and get rid of luxuries like unnecessary furniture, carriages, and the piano. The older children would support themselves or help support the family, while the younger ones would be educated for a life of work and self-reliance. This was an example of Tolstoy's populism, the chief leftist movement in Russia from the 1870s to the 90s when Marxism replaced it. His version of the movement was based on Rousseau's belief in the goodness of the simple life of nature and work as exemplified in Tolstoy's mind by the Russian peasant class. His idealization of it is a theme in *Anna Karenina*, in which Levin, having been initially rejected by Kitty, is tempted to find a peasant bride. Like Olenin in *The Cossacks*, however, Levin learns that to live authentically he must find a gentry version of the simple life. By the 1880s, Tolstoy was ready to become a peasant, or at least his idea of one—someone living a natural, communal existence. Sofya and her older children, to whom Tolstoy was also close, did not agree with this idea, though. He tried hard to convert his family to his way of thinking. He mobilized relatives and the increasing number of his followers who visited the estate to hay, haul manure, and lay bricks. Sofya and her supporters, on the other hand, held their noses and opened windows to let out the smell when the crew returned from such tasks. We know about this and other irritants from memoirs and from the diaries that many members of the household were writing and often sharing with one another. For a while, there was even a post box set up in the household where people could share their opinions, rather as they do today in social media. All annoyances were discussed obsessively as the closeness that had earlier cemented the happy life on the estate now threw up obstacles at it. It did not help either that Sofya was as active and high strung as her husband, and that especially during her (frequent) pregnancies, she was prone to hysteria. Earlier in their marriage, she was Tolstoy's confidant and felt that she was his full partner, as well as the mother of his children, the keeper of his hearth, and the diligent copier of his manuscripts. Back then, she had shared his goals; now, he was asking her to subordinate what she regarded as the interests of the family to utopian ideals she could not embrace. In an ironic twist that Tolstoy seemed not to have noticed, by refusing to yield to her husband's wishes Sofya demonstrated the validity of his belief in individual human freedom as the principle in all consensual relationships. At the same time, like Anna with Vronsky, Sofya had built her life solely around her relationship with her husband, so when he distanced himself from her it felt like an open wound. Her nervousness increased, at times breaking into bouts of mental instability. She began to fear his numerous absences. When he threatened to leave altogether, she would respond with threats of suicide. In his diaries, Tolstoy wavered between pity, anger, guilt, and the futile determination to keep his negative feelings under control. He compromised his new principles multiple times, but this only increased his inner alienation and bitterness. He believed in truth and authenticity above all else, but these virtues made the diplomacy necessary to maintain his marriage impossible. It was a recipe for disaster, and material for the dark dramas of the later period in his life.

In September 1881, the family began to spend winters in Moscow to attend to the educational and social needs of the children; in 1882, Tolstoy bought a house there called Khamovniki after the factory district in which it was located. Built in 1805, it was one of the few wooden structures to survive the burning of Moscow in the War of 1812. (Today the building is a museum.) When Tolstoy purchased the house, it was run down, but he loved the expansive grounds that made him feel as though he were in the country. In 1882, he lived with two of his sons in an outbuilding on the property while he oversaw an extensive renovation and expansion of the main building. He spent parts of his winters in this house (though he also often stayed at Yasnaya Polyana while his family remained in Moscow) until 1901. Though Tolstoy was a countryman at heart and hated city life, he began to explore it. Industrialization with its attendant dislocations of peasants to the city, and its injustice, was in full swing.

Writings on Poverty

Tolstoy participated in the Moscow Census in January 1882. The two works based on this experience chart the radicalization of his thought about the problem of social injustice. The first one, an article entitled "On the Moscow Census" (1882), calls on fellow participants in the scientific work of the census to involve themselves personally in the lives of its subjects, "to remove the immense evil of the separation existing between us and the poor, and to establish relations with them as well as taking up the task of redressing the evil, the misfortunes, the poverty, and our still greater misfortune—the indifference and aimlessness of our lives." This does not mean simply giving money but, rather, rendering direct, hands-on assistance to those in need. The article ends with a call to action: "All together, Brothers, and right away!" The second work, a book written over the next four years entitled *What Then Must We Do?*, revisits the earlier article and corrects it from a much more radical point of view developed by Tolstoy as he tried to implement his first solution. The real problem, as he had already suspected in his first article, was not to be found among the poor, but with the rich. The luxuries they demanded were produced by the working poor, who labored hundreds of hours to manufacture these goods, while earning only a subsistence living in return. At least in the countryside, they support themselves and the wealthy few through meaningful work in nature. But the life desired by the wealthy was only fully attainable in cities, where to support it thousands of workers performed menial mechanical tasks in factories for very little money, while living in substandard housing, which Tolstoy visited during the census and afterward. The rich knew, though they might not have wanted to admit this even to themselves, that their dependence on the poorly compensated labor of others was unjust. Therefore, they had built a wall between themselves and the poor through their way of dressing, their food, their education, even their habits of cleanliness. However, the city poor observed how the wealthy lived, and became corrupted by their indolence, which they desired for themselves. Tolstoy felt ashamed when he handed out alms to the poor; having taken so much from them, he was giving them a pittance back. He noticed that the poor themselves helped the destitute among them, and that, in general, they were not like the wealthy in both their strengths and weaknesses, but actually superior to them. That was because they had to work for a living rather than rely on the labor of others. Money, rather than being the solution to the problems of unjust society, was part of the problem. It undergirded a new, more terrible form of slavery that allowed the wealthy few to steal from the poor without feeling any personal obligation to them. So the solution to injustice that Tolstoy proposed in his second work on the problem of poverty was to abstain from using money, to require for oneself only what was really necessary to sustain life and, to the extent possible, to acquire those things through one's own efforts rather than through the work of others.

Though it was heavily censored and published in full abroad only in 1902 and in Russia in 1906, *What Then Must We Do?* was a bombshell when parts of it appeared in 1886 and in English translation (by Isabel Hapgood) in 1887. In a century in which progress had become a secular religion, the book equated that progress with injustice and even slavery. It appealed to thousands of readers who were uncomfortable with the status quo in industrializing societies for some of the same reasons people today object to globalization. Two of the book's readers were Jane Addams, an American activist and founder of Hull House, a social settlement in Chicago for newly arrived immigrants; and Aylmer Maude, a British businessman who first discovered Tolstoy through the book, and subsequently became his friend, biographer, and translator. In a 1935 introduction to his 1925 translation of *What Then Must We Do?*, Maude recalled that though he and other readers found Tolstoy's critique of the situation over-simplified and overly logical, it was spell-binding in its moral clarity. Some questioned Tolstoy's sincerity about his radical proposals because he did not practice what he preached. Maude explained that Tolstoy did not take up the life of simple labor he recommended in the work because his wife, whom he loved, would not allow it. This makes sense if we keep in mind Sofya's threats of suicide if he abandoned her and the family.

Notes of a Madman

The move to the city had created yet another discord in relations between the Tolstoys. For Sofya, who had spent the first two decades of married life mostly closeted at Yasnaya Polyana, it was a chance to participate in society life as a still young and attractive woman and the wife of a famous author. She and her sociable 18-year-old daughter Tatyana took full advantage of this opportunity. Meanwhile, her husband called for an end to the way of life that she and Tatyana were enjoying for the first time. They held dinners and soirees while he was trying to give up smoking, drinking, hunting, meat, and even tea. He learned how to make shoes (though not very well), so he could do something useful, but he was no longer concerned about supporting himself or his family; Sofya, meanwhile, worried about educating the children and about paying for life in the city. In 1883, as a concession to her money worries, Tolstoy signed over to her the legal right to conduct his business affairs. In 1885, she undertook the publication of his collected works herself, and this became the family's primary source of income. (Between 1886 and 1891, she published eight different editions of his works.) Maude reported that when Tolstoy wanted to take all his writings out of copyright and make them free to the public, Sofya threatened "to appeal to the Tsar to have her husband declared incapable of disposing of his property." As a compromise, he gave his wife the exclusive right to sell works written before 1881, as well as occasional works of fiction written since then. She continued to scramble to obtain the first publications of later works for her editions, and quarrels over these money issues poisoned their life together. The stress between the two was huge, and Tolstoy began to fantasize about escaping it. Already in 1882, Sofya reported in her diary that he had shouted about wanting to leave her. In 1884, he did leave home, but returned for the birth of their fourth daughter, Aleksandra.

Between 1884 and 1886, in the midst of all this turmoil, Tolstoy borrowed from his earlier experience at Arzamas to work on a story he called *Notes of a Madman*. The way he did this is a significant example of how he mined his life for his art without being tied to his biography. When he had originally reported his Arzamas terror in a letter to his wife in 1869, it was clear that he attributed his *toska* to being on the road and away from her and the family. In *Notes*, a first-person narrator cures the spiritual anguish that others label as madness by embracing religion, reading Holy Scripture, and rejecting the family way of life that Tolstoy had so desperately missed in his original tender letter to Sofya. All these elements reflected his state of mind in the mid-1880s. By then, as we know, he was tearing up plank by plank (both literally and figuratively) the life that he had built with Sofya over the past 25 years. He was also writing *The Death of Ivan Ilych*.

The Death of Ivan Ilych

This masterpiece, published in 1886, can be read in two ways that are related but not the same. Most obviously, it is a social satire. One critic (Edward Wasiolek) said that Tolstoy put the funeral of the title character first in order to alienate the reader from him in the account of his life to follow. In this scenario, the first chapter is a vignette, or illustration, of how Ivan must have lived his life. To some extent, this chapter already justifies the narrator's harsh treatment of Ivan, who would have treated others the same way.

The story comments implicitly on Russian legal reforms in the 1860s. Ivan Ilych is a "new man," one of the lawyers who in the new system oversee justice in Russian society. This backdrop does not jump out at us now, and therefore we are much more likely to read the work outside its historical context, as a satire on bureaucracy in general. It debunks the life of upper-middle-class government bureaucrats, with their pretension, mediocrity, and conventionality. There are a number of German names among the cast of characters, and Tolstoy's Germans tend to be phlegmatic, rationalistic, self-centered, and conformist. The merry, egocentric character who winks at Ivan's acquaintance Pyotr Ivanovich and sneaks away before the service to play cards is named Schwartz.

Tolstoy accomplishes this satire through an Enlightenment technique that the formalist critic Viktor Shklovsky dubbed "making strange" [*ostranenie*]. One of the main purposes of art, according to Shklovsky, is to unfamiliarize us with things that make sense to us simply because we are so used to them and accept them without thinking. Shklovsky pointed out that several hundred such passages appear in Tolstoy's work. He also said that Tolstoy did not use *ostranenie* just to expose the negative side of things—it can be positive as well. It grows out of Tolstoy's interest in and use of point of view. In *War and Peace*, for instance, when Pierre courts Natasha, he views everything through the lens of his love for her; that would fit Shklovsky's definition of *ostranenie*. He demonstrated how a situation that makes sense to insiders—like the reaction of Ivan Ilych's colleagues to the news of his death—is senseless when looked at "objectively," from the point of view of an outsider. Tolstoy himself, in his later work *The Kingdom of God Is Within You* (1890-93), associated this technique with the story about the child who is the only one who sees that the Emperor has no clothes.

The Death of Ivan Ilych is built from the ground up by *ostranenie*. First, the narrator gives us the story of the title character's life from Ivan's point of view, and then Ivan himself makes his past life "strange," so that by the end of the story he rejects his own characterization of it as "pleasant and proper." Beyond that, however, we can see that the narrator intervenes in the first recounting of Ivan's story so as to discredit his life. He makes it "strange" by beginning with the account of the reaction of those in Ivan's milieu. He then tells Ivan's story in such a way as to keep us from identifying with him.

Contemporary readers of *The Death of Ivan Ilych* who understood the story from the narrator's perspective shared his moral indignation as he looked down on foolish and venal characters. The Soviets read it as an exposé of the Russian upper classes that they had overthrown. For them, the peasant servant Gerasim, with his kindliness and his straightforward acceptance of death, is an example of the attitude of the exploited class under the Tsarist regime. Other readers, however, have seen the work as a kind of satire on life itself. Drawing a connection between this book and Tolstoy's later work, *Confession* (1882), they perceive Ivan Ilych as a stand-in for Tolstoy himself. In *Confession*, Tolstoy spoke of the spiritual crisis that came over him in the middle of his life using the simile of a man who, like Ivan Ilych, discovers that he has a fatal disease.

> There occurred what occurred with everyone sick with a deadly internal disease. At first, there appear trivial signs of indisposition to which the sick man pays no attention, then these signs reappear more and more often and merge into one ceaseless suffering. This suffering grows and, before the sick man can glance back, he becomes aware that what he took for an indisposition is what is for him more important than anything else in the world—death.

This approach to *The Death of Ivan Ilych* puts readers in a less comfortable position. If it is social satire, we look down on attendees at the viewing of the body as complacent booboisie, the upper-middle classes we despise. But in the same opening chapter, the narrator remarks that people at the wake react "as always" to the death of others by thinking: it happens to him, not to me. The appeal to universal behaviors and sentiments is the very technique that Tolstoy used to get readers to identify with his characters. We don't have a direct line into the feelings of others except by analogy to our own. The use of universal maxims continues as the narrator states authoritatively that, "like everyone else on such occasions," Pyotr Ivanovich uneasily looks around to see what everyone else is doing. Here we, the readers, identify with Pyotr Ivanovich, and it is through his eyes that we view the body. Once again, Tolstoy appealed, brutally this time, to our own experience of such things. He made us look at dead human flesh, and we empathize with Pyotr Ivanovich as he hurriedly leaves the room. Then later, Tolstoy allowed Pyotr Ivanovich to rise to the level of self-consciousness in which, as he imagines Ivan Ilych's suffering, he senses his own hypocrisy. He pushes away his horror with another "customary reflection," that "this had happened to Ivan Ilych, and not to him and that it ought not and could not happen to him." At the end of Chapter 6, when we find him "not yielding to the gloomy impression," we understand why.

Thus, readers are forced by a relentless narrator to confront our defensive feelings about death. But in our earlier, secure position, we perceived Pyotr Ivanovich as a double for Ivan Ilych. So, we too are like Ivan Ilych, and we too will follow his story—not with the smug satisfaction that he is that petty bourgeois lawyer, but with the trembling feeling that he is "I." To philosophize, in Tolstoy's opinion, we must confront death as the great destroyer of all our attempts to create order in the world. It is this radical impulse to face up to all our taboos, even those surrounding death, that drives the later Tolstoy. He had, by this time, discovered rituals and behaviors that help humans cope with death, and he makes them strange.

To philosopher Leo Shestov, *The Death of Ivan Ilych* was primarily about the human condition, not just a satire on civilization, and the protagonist is Everyman.

> Proprieties: that is how Tolstoy designates everything that we are accustomed to calling social and cosmic order, the world common to all waking men, to which Aristotle opposed the individual worlds of those who slept and dreamed. Is the dying man just such a dreamer, only one who is being torn against his will from the world common to all? ("The Last Judgement: Tolstoy's Last Works," from *In Job's Balances*, 1929)

In tone, the chronicle of Ivan Ilych's life up to the time of his illness is like a court transcript as told by the protagonist, but emotionally flat, with the narrator taking no emotional part in the recitation of facts that include Ivan Ilych's values. But the tone changes when the narrative shifts to the detailed inner story of the illness and death of the protagonist. Whereas before readers saw his life from outside, now we see the world in which Ivan Ilych has lived from his point of view as his illness drives a wedge between the world and himself.

The setting of the story is all interiors, with no reference to the outdoors or nature, except for the smell of it on Gerasim's clothing. Ivan Ilych gets in touch with reality only through his suffering, which eventually directs him to inner voices that have been silenced throughout his adult life. In this sense, his illness plays a salutary role, and nothing becomes his life like the ending of it.

At death, Ivan Ilych is alone. He has dismissed Gerasim, and, although he pities and forgives his family, he does not want them to know that. This fact signaled his creator's turning away from intimacy with loved ones as a way to overcome the problems of individual mortality. And the great writer who celebrated physical vitality had now turned on it as an obstacle to spirituality. Like Andrey in *War and Peace*, Ivan Ilych also perceives his own death as good; in his case, as birth into a better, more enlightened world.

The Kreutzer Sonata

In the period between the publication of *The Death of Ivan Ilych* and the writing of *The Kreutzer Sonata*, Tolstoy's relations with his wife, family, and the government remained strained. He continued to try to get his bad habits under control. In 1888, he gave up smoking for good, and he wanted to translate a book by American doctor Alice B. Stockham, *Tocology, A Book for Every Woman* (Chicago, 1888), which advocates "controlled intercourse" within marriage as a way to avoid unwanted pregnancies. (He wrote an introduction to the Russian translation, which was published in 1892.) Tolstoy was not practicing this method himself, however: Ivan, his 13th and last child, was born in 1888 when he was 60 years old, and according to her biographer Nina Nikitina, Sofya miscarried another pregnancy in 1890. He wrote a series of works that reflect his struggles with sex at the time. These works include *The Devil* (1889), *Father Sergius* (begun in 1890 and worked on intermittently until 1898), and *The Kreutzer Sonata*.

In both *The Devil* and *Father Sergius*, a demonic female seduces the protagonist. This woman—sensuous and earthy—resembles Anna Karenina, as Tolstoy originally imagined her. In the novel, however, erotic love acquired a higher function than mere sensuality, and Anna evolved into the complex character partly to reflect that. In

Tolstoy's works from the late 1880s, erotic love is associated exclusively with Dionysian crimes. In one ending of *The Devil*, the married landowner hero kills himself; in the other, he murders his peasant lover. In *Father Sergius*, the protagonist is an ambitious military officer, Prince Stepan Kasatsky, who has ties to the court in St. Petersburg. He reveres Tsar Nicholas I, the patron of his elite cadet school, but when he discovers that his fiancée has been the Tsar's lover, he becomes a monk named Father Sergius. His reputation as a holy man and healer spreads, and a man asks Sergius to cure his daughter, believed to be possessed by devilish lust. But Kasatsky/Sergius succumbs to lust himself and has sex with the girl. Afterward, he runs away to become a wandering beggar, without even a name. One wonders whether his creator, Tolstoy, now a very famous author, was not fantasizing about doing the same thing.

Of the novellas about sex that Tolstoy worked on in the 1880s, the most complex and the only one published in his lifetime was *The Kreutzer Sonata*. (*The Devil* and *Father Sergius* were published posthumously, and another one developed into his third novel, *Resurrection*.) *The Kreutzer Sonata* is a story within a story, in which the protagonist, Pozdnyshev, tells the frame narrator how he murdered his wife because he was convinced she was having an affair with a violinist named Trukhachevsky. The title of the story refers to Beethoven's Violin Sonata No. 9, with its intimate dialogue between the piano and the violin. The wife (whose name we never learn) and Trukhachevsky play this piece at a dinner party arranged by Pozdnyshev. The graphic description of the murder is shocking. The work is autobiographical in the sense that Tolstoy drew upon his own conflicted feelings about his wife and marriage. It goes without saying that Sofya was deeply offended by it. Unwisely, she wrote a fictional response to it entitled *Who is to Blame? (Regarding The Kreutzer Sonata)*. In it, an older prince marries an innocent 18-year-old girl and deflowers her in a covered coach on the wedding trip to his estate. (As readers will recall, this episode is a reference to the Tolstoys' own marriage.) Ten years later, an older and wiser wife has an intense, platonic friendship with a former neighbor. They are about to separate—he is dying of tuberculosis—but when she returns from a farewell drive, her husband kills her in a fit of jealous rage with a marble paperweight. Only after she dies, does he start appreciating her purity, and all she has done for him. Sofya did not publish this thinly veiled autobiographical fantasy, though she did read it from time to time to others. When a separate publication of *The Kreutzer Sonata* was banned for its raw naturalism, however, she was determined to include it in the collected works she oversaw. After traveling to St. Petersburg for a personal interview with the Tsar arranged by Alexandrine Tolstaya, she received special permission to do this. Her husband was not happy about her petition because he considered it kowtowing to authority. The work came out separately in 1900, and in an uncensored version only in 1933, in the Academy edition of Tolstoy's works.

The Kreutzer Sonata comments on contemporary attitudes about women and marriage. It begins with a first-person narrator on a train chatting about love with fellow travelers from traditional and modern milieus. An old merchant agrees with the government and church that sexual desire needs to be harnessed for the sake of family and society. He is hypocritical because he gets to philander while women cannot; furthermore, he wants to keep women in their place through force. A liberated woman and a lawyer—the latter a defender of law rather than morality—argue for free love as beneficial for individuals. Pozdnyshev overhears this conversation and introduces himself as the perpetrator of a sensational murder that he assumes everyone has heard about. When he is alone with the narrator, he relates the crime and its causes as he understands them. Blaming the sexualized culture of the upper classes, and especially the treatment of women as sex objects, he recommends abstinence even within marriage. Readers were scandalized by the story and this point especially. But they also reacted favorably to open discussions of this important issue of the day that others were afraid to talk about. The story resonated with many women.

In his rants, Pozdnyshev makes romantic love strange. He argues that it is nothing more than physical attraction and love of power; therefore, it can't be the basis of marriage, because it can't succeed in permanently conquering the beloved except, perhaps, by killing her. Marriage should be, but is not, a contract with God, a religious covenant based on friendship. As Pozdnyshev sees it, he murdered his wife because he believed that he owned her body and soul, and she resisted this. The plunging of a knife into her portrayed with such detail suggests the sex act, which, as in the depiction of the consummation of the affair of Anna and Vronsky, is seen as a kind of murder. Pozdnyshev emphasizes that the relationship with the violinist was only a pretext for killing his wife, whom he already hated. This is why he let the lover into his house, even though he immediately sensed the potential for adultery and jealousy, and he allowed the concert in which his wife and the violinist played the Kreutzer Sonata to go forward. He also insists in his confession that every step of the murder, once he resolved upon it, was premeditated, and he was conscious of what he was doing at every moment. It was a calculated act performed under the influence of revenge and hatred.

Readers shocked by the extremity of Pozdnyshev's views wanted to believe that the author did not embrace these same radical opinions, and there is something to this. Tolstoy wrote an Afterword to the story that defended celibacy even in marriage—and hence the end of the human race—but only as a theoretical ideal, not as something realistic. To deliver his double message, Tolstoy chose a setting and a frame narrator that implicitly distanced the author from the apocalyptical zeal of Pozdnyshev's views, but not from the adoption of these beliefs as a goal. The story is also full of symbolism: Pozdnyshev tells it on a train, a symbol for Tolstoy of unharnessed energy in the industrial age, and of the attempt to conquer nature to serve human greed and love of power. When Pozdnyshev, who is away from home, receives his wife's letter telling him that she has been seeing Trukhachevsky, he is able to rush to commit the murder because he can catch a train. When traveling from his estate to the train station in the traditional way, by carriage, he enjoys the night and nature and is distracted from his intent, while the noise of the lunging pistons and the speed of the train inflame his passion so much that he blames the train ride (among other things) for his crime.

As described by the frame narrator, Pozdnyshev is short with gleaming eyes and curly, prematurely gray hair. Chain-smoking and drinking very strong tea, eyes darting, he moves around constantly. He is preoccupied, and makes a peculiar noise, maybe a laugh, maybe a sob, apparently in response to new thoughts as they keep occurring to him. As he makes his key argument for the end of sex, even in marriage, he asks the narrator to cover the lamp so that it is dark. Pozdnyshev agrees it was right for his wife's sister and brother to take his children away from him, saying, "I am a wreck, a cripple. There is one thing in me. I know. Yes, it is true that I know what others will not soon find out." Like Prince Andrey before Borodino, Pozdnyshev, too, has learned truths that make life impossible, and that can be embraced only by a man like him. The argument is sick, unnatural, and hence given to a sick man. And yet Tolstoy thinks it has merit. Pozdnyshev's argument for celibacy is cynical on the one hand, and idealistic on the other, with both states of mind being products of his extreme alienation from normal life. He knows, but he is not in a reasonable, reflective state. The candle, a symbol of reason, goes out on the train as he describes the murder, and only his "more and more agitated suffering voice" is heard. This is a story of darkness told in darkness, and Pozdnyshev probably repeats it incessantly to everyone he meets. It is part confession, part excuse, and, from the point of view of Tolstoy as author, part truth.

The Kreutzer Sonata is also about art. Music, according to Pozdnyshev, takes listeners (or performers) out of themselves, either elevating the soul or lowering it. Since it puts listeners in such a receptive mood, it should also guide them. He says a work of this power should be played only on grand occasions, aimed at particular results on which to expend the energy aroused by the music. This argument is related to Tolstoy's idea of how art functions: the recipient of it is "infected" by the feelings of the artist expressed in his work.

In *The Kreutzer Sonata* the dangers of "infection" are suggested. The recipient is in an exposed position, out of himself and open to the influence of others. Hence music can make him yawn when he is not sleepy and laugh when there is nothing to laugh about. Understood this way, art is clearly related to sex and eros: readers will recall how Vronsky is "infected" by Anna's moods when he first falls in love with her. And we can also connect this argument to sexual feeling as Pozdnyshev describes it. It is arousal of unfocused energy for the purpose of bodily pleasure. This is a far cry from the idea of eros as depicted in earlier works. There, it could be harnessed to ideals that direct the individual toward the good. Here, as Pozdnyshev portrays it, this is all nonsense, used to hide the underlying dynamics of gratification of an animal appetite or, worse, love of power.

Art is dangerous, but even in *The Kreutzer Sonata* it is not depicted as all bad. Although the murder is associated with musical terms like "crescendo," it is significant that the performance of the sonata arouses only positive feelings, not only in the musicians, but also in Pozdnyshev himself. And this is true even though he observes a blissful intimacy between the performers that suggests sexual fulfillment. Presumably, this intimacy is what he desired and did not achieve with his wife, and Tolstoy the artist still desires it with his readers. In and of itself, such intimacy is a good thing, but the artist must take responsibility for guiding the feelings he arouses in the recipient. Thus, Tolstoy hoped that his work would encourage marriage based on higher, brotherly love, rather than the lower, sensual kind, and he was disturbed when readers did not react the same way.

5. A New Path

In the 1880s, Tolstoy began to distance himself from old friends. In the 1860s and 70s, Fet and his wife had been among the very few non-relatives invited to Yasnaya Polyana. Tolstoy often corresponded with him about literature and philosophy. In 1869, he proposed to Fet a joint translation of Schopenhauer's *The World as Will and Idea*; Fet did translate it, but without Tolstoy's collaboration. In 1879, in the midst of his religious searches, Tolstoy recommended that Fet read Ecclesiastes because this book of the Hebrew Bible "has much in common with Schopenhauer." In October 1880, the two exchanged letters about Tolstoy's new religious ideas, with Fet refuting them. The following year, their correspondence ended, even though Fet lived until 1892 and they continued to see each other. Although he did not break with her entirely, Tolstoy also quarreled with Alexandrine Tolstaya about the path he was taking. Nikolay Strakhov (1828-1896), a public intellectual and prolific author of articles and books mapping the Russian philosophical terrain and with whom Tolstoy had been close since Strakhov had written a set of essays on *War and Peace*, remained a friend, but one with a diminished influence on him.

In *The Death of Ivan Ilych*, the protagonist dies. In *The Kreutzer Sonata*, the life of the main character, Pozdnyshev, is over, even though he is not dead. His surname, which means "late" in Russian, indicates that he discovers the truth of his situation too late to rectify it. Tolstoy, the author of these two works, lived for over two decades after completing them. As he explained in *Confession*, he, like many of his contemporaries, thought life was meaningless, but went on living, seemingly because he lacked the courage to commit suicide. There were better reasons to stay alive, at least according to Tolstoy as guru and preacher, and *Confession* is the story of how he discovered this truth.

Confession

This seminal work relates the author's life story from the point of view of his new beliefs. In it, he recounted how he rejected religion as a teenager, and replaced it with the goal of what he calls self-perfectivization. Later this turned into a belief in progress that he acquired from the intelligentsia with whom he fraternized in the 1850s in St. Petersburg. He soon came to doubt progress as a moral goal, but marriage and happy family life then delayed an inevitable crisis of faith for 15 years. When it arrived, Tolstoy staved off despair for a while by embracing the Russian Orthodox faith practiced by other members of his family and by Russian peasants. Though the superstitions and irrational rituals woven into its doctrine bothered him, what he found most off-putting—and what ultimately led him to reject this path—were the dogmas and intolerance of the Church hierarchy and intelligentsia.

In her book "*Who, What Am I?*": *Tolstoy Struggles to Narrate the Self* (2014), Irina Paperno identified *Confession* as a conversion tale in the tradition of Rousseau, St. Augustine, and others. As such, it is a first-person narrative, and purportedly in the voice of the author himself. What is important for understanding Tolstoy's poetics and the relation between his life and works is how stylized the narrative is, and how, rather than recounting Tolstoy's life as it actually occurred, it serves his present purposes. As in *The Death of Ivan Ilych*, he emptied the life story of the title character (in this case, purportedly himself) of meaning in order to build up the conversion and its aftermath as an escape from meaninglessness. For instance, he claimed to have been an atheist in the 1850s, but the supposed non-believer at that time required the ideal reader of *Childhood* to be "religious," and in 1855 he recorded in his diary a desire to found a new religion. The narrator of *Confession* claims in Chapter 2 to have begun to write "from vanity, greed, and pride" "to get glory and money." To achieve this goal, he needed "to hide the good and to display the bad" in himself and especially to hide "those strivings of mine towards goodness which gave meaning to my life." When he was in crisis, art, as noted in Chapter 4, seemed to him to be nothing but "a decoration to life, an enticement to life."

But Tolstoy was never simply the fame-seeking, money-grubbing, selfish aesthete depicted in *Confession*. This definition and all the other demeaning criticism in *Confession* came from the same author who, as he began *Anna Karenina*, on April 7, 1873, wrote his wife that "I am fulfilling a duty laid upon me by some most high command—I am in torment, and I find in this torment the whole, not joy, but goal of life." He always sought meaning in his life, and art for him had a high moral purpose. *Confession* hints at this, when, describing art as a "mirror" of life, the narrator says that he can no longer produce it, because when he looks into that mirror now, all he sees is that "my position was stupid and desperate." In that sense, one can even regard Tolstoy's crisis as precipitating a search for a meaning that had made art possible for him earlier, and must do the same now. He knew he was a great writer—in Chapter 3, he compared himself with utter confidence to Pushkin, Gogol, Shakespeare, and Molière—and he accepted the burden that this imposed. He also knew that the modes of art, the "comic, tragic, touching, fine, and terrible," only exist as expressions of the higher meaning that art conveys through them.

Once he falls into crisis, the narrator of *Confession* looks to "science" for the meaning he is seeking. This word in Russian [*nauka*] has a broader meaning than in modern English, including both the study of the material world and of philosophy. The two are joined, according to Tolstoy, by their reliance on human reason. Natural science and math produce clear results in their investigations of matter, but cannot attribute spiritual meaning to the life of a human individual who, according to them, is merely a conglomeration of particles that come together for a while and then separate. The philosophical sciences as practiced by the wisest men in different cultures—Socrates, Schopenhauer, Solomon, Indian wisdom as encapsulated in the story of Shakyamuni—all reach the same conclusions as the narrator himself, namely, that life is vanity and, therefore, the wise man welcomes death as a release from it.

The narrator's solution to his dilemma is a Kantian one, according to which the infinite is inaccessible to human reason (even if the infinite itself on some level might be reasonable), and therefore faith, as practiced by all human societies, is the necessary conduit to the infinite from the finite. From this, he concludes that the pessimism of great philosophers is merely a recognition that philosophy asks the right question—what is the meaning of life?—but cannot answer it. In claiming that he only now frees himself from enslavement to human reason, he once again misrepresents his past life. This is the author who in *War and Peace* stated that life would be impossible if it were merely reasonable (Epilogue, Part 1, Chapter 1), and who, through his surrogate Levin in *Anna Karenina*, had already made an argument about science similar to the one in *Confession*.

The narrator of *Confession*, like Ivan Ilych, sees himself as returning to the unself-conscious point of view of childhood, though now he embraces it self-consciously and wants to disentangle it from the irrationalities and corruptions of truth in which tradition had packaged it. I leave it to philosophers to judge the value of Tolstoy's thoughts here. Certainly, they are not original, but they represent two profound elements of his world view. The first is his fundamental conviction, held from the beginning, that human beings have reason and cannot take a single step without assuming, either explicitly or implicitly, that what they are doing is both explicable and good. So, in Volume 2, Part 2, of *War and Peace*, after Pierre Bezukhov has wounded his wife's lover Dolokhov in a duel, he questions the presuppositions of his life that led to this dreadful outcome. As he does this, his life stops. Tolstoy's narrator expresses this state as a breakdown in the machinery of Pierre's mind. It is as if, he says, a screw has been stripped and keeps turning rather than holding the mind together and in working order. Pierre is rescued from chaos and provided with a new set of moral principles by his mentor, Freemason Osip Bazdeev. In the same way, the narrator of *Confession* searches for meaning so that he can live.

What changed in this stage of Tolstoy's life was his solution to the quest for meaning of the mortal, lonely self. Whereas before he had sought it in loving relations with other human beings, he now turned inward to search for it in his relationship with God. There is a direct line in *Confession* between this solution and his loss of his mother. In an astonishingly revealing metaphor, he imagines himself as a fledgling fallen from the nest and God as the mother who embraces and cares for him. When he joins his mortal self with infinity in this way, he is at one with the infinite Whole, but, paradoxically, he is farther from intimacy with other human beings than he has ever been. The state of mind he now advocates resembles that of Platon Karataev. As Pierre observes about Platon, he has perfect judgment and gets along with everyone, but is not close to anyone. The narrator of *Confession* also aspires to the aloofness, the closeness to God, and the resultant perfect judgment of a Platon. How every individual might achieve this state, and what that person's judgment might be on different issues, becomes the subject of Tolstoy's late non-fictional works, many of which, significantly, are written in the first person and relate episodes from the narrator's life.

Other Works

Tolstoy originally tried (though unsuccessfully) to publish *Confession* under the title *Introduction to an Unpublished Work*. It was intended to introduce *An Investigation of Dogmatic Theology* (1879-81, 1884), in which, referencing the thought of contemporary theologian Metropolitan Makarius of Moscow, he addressed the doctrines that alienated him from the Church. In addition to problems of religious toleration, these include most prominently the Church reserving for itself direct connection to God, and denying it to individuals. He then rewrote the Gospels to purge them of what he saw as inconsistencies and corruptions

(*Translation and Harmony of the Four Gospels*). (He studied Hebrew with a Moscow Rabbi to do this.) Finally, he wrote *What I Believe* (1882-1884), in which he explained his purpose in *An Investigation of Dogmatic Theology* and his rewriting of the Gospels, laid out his new beliefs, and recommended them to all.

What I Believe

This work begins with the observation that at the time of its writing, some 1800 years after Christ preached, no Christian society was following his core precepts. Using his own case as a stand-in for all, Tolstoy attributed this paradox to the effects of miseducation, habit, and an "animal" need for the approval of others. He noted several times in Chapter 5 that "strangely," it had been his lot to discover the true teaching of Christ. The confessional form of the work was intended to provide an example for readers to follow, and also indirectly to defend the author against attacks for the sin of pride at his accomplishment.

Once again, the narrator empties his earlier life of all meaning, going even further in this respect than he had done in *Confession*. He claims that before, he was a nihilist "in the sense of being completely without faith," and he compares himself to the thief on the cross who is saved by embracing Christ's message. Once he has done this, he undertakes a scholarly journey to extract that message from corrupted and still misunderstood texts. Christ builds his teaching on the law already enunciated in the Old Testament: that one should love one's neighbor as oneself. It is striking that Tolstoy conceded in Chapter 6 the impossibility of loving one's enemies. But whereas Jews consider only other Jews to be "neighbors," Christians must love people of all nations and ethnicities. Though Tolstoy did not develop this theme in *What I Believe*, it underlies his rejection of war in his later life.

Furthermore, Christ replaced the "eye for an eye" mentality of

Mosaic law with what Tolstoy called the principle of "non-resistance to evil." The only way to have a non-violent, just society is not to repay violence with violence, and not to judge lest you yourself be judged. This means that the whole judicial system, from law enforcement to courts to prisons, is inherently unjust. From non-resistance to evil, Tolstoy deduced other principles, including a prohibition against oaths, and one against military service. He said that Christ called for the suppression of all anger and vengeance, even when they seemed justified, as well as for forgiveness of the anger and foolishness of others. Christ also cautioned against abandoning one's wife and the temptation of lust. Anger and lust, in Tolstoy's psychology, were the great enemies of reason in the soul, and these last commandments were meant to moderate them. All the commandments—expressed most concisely, in Tolstoy's opinion, in the Sermon on the Mount—lead to the very Tolstoyan conclusion, that "not a single person has any rights and can be lower or higher than another, that only the person who tries to rise above all others is lower and more degraded than others." In the Gospels, Tolstoy saw an attack on the pride and love of power that, in his opinion, underlay all political systems. Christ also left an example by his life of non-resistance that, if followed, would lead toward the annihilation of evil within society.

Christ, as Tolstoy represented him, was a prophet of God, tasked with moving human society closer to divine law. Although Tolstoy never directly said this, he may have also considered himself a prophet, though of lesser importance than Christ. But like Christ, he may have been updating religion in a way that moved it ever closer to "the true eternal law of God." The results of his scholarly exegesis of the Gospels and earlier commentaries on them seem "Tolstoyan." At the very least, he made them relevant to modern times. Perhaps the most striking in this regard was his abolition of the tension between reason and revelation. In Chapter 7, he insisted on the equation of God and reason and, consequently, the logic in Christ's teachings, as expressed in his sermons and parables. One example out of many is his interpretation of the "miracle" of the loaves and fishes in Chapter 10, in which he posited that Christ did not miraculously multiply the supplies; instead, he convinced the masses to share everything they brought, and there was food for all.

Tolstoy argued that the history of humankind consists of the struggle between our animal and our rational natures, and moral progress requires that we take the side of reason. Not just Christ, but all wise teachers of humanity have preached this doctrine. God helps those who help themselves: this is the essence of Christianity, according to Tolstoy. In order to turn our backs on our animal selves, we must fully acknowledge our mortality and the futility of all our attempts to evade it. Only then will we be able to embrace the infinite over the finite (Chapter 8) and give up our individual lives to serve the lives of all. Christ did this, and Tolstoy insisted that he truly became mortal and truly died to do it.

In Tolstoy's view, therefore, Christ was not resurrected. Christianity follows Judaism in seeing individuals as mortal, and corrects it in extending eternity not just to the Chosen People, but to all. Tolstoy's theology is psychologically understandable in his own terms because the individual sacrifices his individual desires and passions to address the most pressing of them: the fear of death and the need to avoid it. "Faith," as Christ (according to Tolstoy) defined it, "is based only on the rational consciousness of what is best in a particular situation [...] on the consciousness of inevitable death, and of the sole salvation possible in this situation" (Chapter 9). It expresses itself, not through belief in the irrational, but through good works. If we all perform these works, Tolstoy claimed, we will still die–and, in that sense, suffer–but the suffering will be minimized.

On Life

In the late 1880s, Tolstoy wrote a philosophical treatise called *On Life*. Rejecting contemporary science and materialist philosophy, he claimed that all knowledge originates in an element of human subjectivity that he called "reasonable consciousness." (He used the term in the quote above from *What I Believe*.) Its appearance within an individual seems at first to bring only suffering. This moment is recorded in *Confession* when the narrator rejects his earlier life and even contemplates suicide. But, Tolstoy pointed out in *On Life*, the person who lives according to the dictates of reasonable consciousness is like a bird who starts to use his wings rather than his feet (Chapter 8). Reason, as the cause of all human cognition as well as the organization of the material world, remains outside the realm of human knowledge (Chapter 10), but only its manifestation in the soul as reasonable consciousness distinguishes us from other animals and makes us fully human (Chapter 7). This does not mean that we are simply reasonable. Just as he had believed all his life, Tolstoy conceded that we are composite beings made up of bodies, feelings, mind, and will. Our reasonable consciousness can only govern our animal self, not replace it. Only this consciousness can answer the question of how each one of us should live our life. So in this sense at least, it is me, while my feelings and body are outside my control, and therefore not me. One of the most striking things about this treatise is how powerful the author considered our animal self to be. Our lives, he implicitly conceded, are made up of the struggle between it and our reason. As animals, we seek pleasure and avoid pain and suffering; only the impossibility of achieving that goal tips the scales in favor of reason.

There is something subdued and depressing about Tolstoy's late philosophy as expressed in *On Life* and elsewhere. No matter how much he insisted that the life of reasonable consciousness is joyous, no one, it seems, could be induced to lead it if it were not for the shadow of death looming over all our pleasures. It is no surprise, therefore, that the first title of his treatise was *On Life and Death*. It may be significant as well that Tolstoy wrote the work after he had suffered an extremely painful and life-threatening bacterial infection in his leg. His need to counter his fear of death in the 1880s intensified, leading to attitudes that seem bizarre. For instance, the man whose life was shaped by his reactions to the death of his loved ones now claimed that one should not mourn death. Thus, when his-four-year-old son Aleksey died 36 hours after a complication of tonsillitis in January 1886, Tolstoy wrote a friend that "the death of a child, which used to seem to me incomprehensible and cruel, now seems to me to be reasonable and good. We've all been joined together more lovingly and closely than before." (It is this hard-heartedness in the name of preserving the idea of God as good that Shestov criticized in his long essay, "The Good in the Teaching of Tolstoy and Nietzsche: Philosophy and Preaching" [1900].) In *On Life*, Tolstoy equated reason itself with the good, and saw the task of reasonable consciousness as directing the animal self toward this good. This is the most controversial element of his philosophy because it required him to assert that the world and life itself are naturally good. He felt, therefore, that he must somehow defend the necessity and goodness of all human suffering, which requires us to take responsibility for all the injustices that befall us. The arguments of this sort in the latter chapters of the treatise are hard to swallow in the light of terrible misfortune of the sort that strikes Ivan Ilych, let alone the manmade horrors of the 20th and now the 21st centuries.

A New Group of Friends

Even as he was rejecting his old life, Tolstoy was assembling the pieces for a new one. This was true in his personal life as well as in his writings. He began to make new friends supportive of the new life he was creating. In 1882, having read "On the Moscow Census," Nikolay Ge, a famous painter, traveled to Moscow to meet its author. He became a follower of Tolstoy, and a friend of the whole Tolstoy family until his death in 1894. Anti-materialist philosopher Nikolay Grot became a close intellectual friend. Pavel Biriukov, another new friend and collaborator, had left the navy because he did not approve of war. Biriukov eventually wrote a biography of Tolstoy. The most important new friend, however, was Vladimir Chertkov. Born in 1854, the tall, handsome son of high nobility close to the court—rumor even had it that he was the illegitimate son of Tsar Alexander II—he was destined for a brilliant military or administrative career. In 1881, however, he resigned his military commission because of his growing conviction that military life was unchristian. He moved to his family estate, where he occupied himself with bettering the lives of local peasants. At their first meeting in 1883, Tolstoy was finishing *What I Believe* and read part of it—in which he condemned military service—to Chertkov. The meeting was a milestone for both of them. Chertkov felt his spiritual isolation had ended, and he became Tolstoy's loyal follower, while in Chertkov Tolstoy had found a disciple from a younger generation. Chertkov was not a sycophant; on the contrary, in their long friendship, the two did occasionally disagree, usually about the implications of Tolstoyanism. Chertkov was a man of action who was more Tolstoyan and certainly less doubting than Tolstoy himself. He was the leader of Tolstoy's admirers whom Sofya took to calling "dark," because she found them so sinister and benighted. At times, he would advise Tolstoy about his writing, and usually Tolstoy did not take that advice. But his practical savvy, connections, and advice were invaluable, and the Tolstoy movement benefited immeasurably from them.

No one in Tolstoy's later circle of friends was more controversial than Chertkov. He was a difficult man, vain, and hard to work with. He loved luxury, and this made people accuse him of hypocrisy. He also loved power and wanted exclusive control over the life and actions of the master. The friendship between the two was intense. Sofya liked him at first, but came to resent his influence on her husband bitterly and even suggested that the two had a sexual relationship. (She based her suspicions about Tolstoy's possible homosexual leanings on the passage in his early diaries about his feelings for his friend and neighbor, Dyakov.) The sons tended to support their mother in her battles with Chertkov, while the second daughter Marya, and especially the youngest one Aleksandra, who did not get along with their mother, eventually supported their father and Chertkov. The oldest daughter Tatyana tried to reconcile the warring parties. Chertkov lived long enough to negotiate Tolstoy's legacy with the new Soviet regime after the revolution, and he was editor-in-chief (and instigator) of the Jubilee edition of Tolstoy's works.

Intermediary

In 1884, Tolstoy and Chertkov, with the cooperation of young publishing entrepreneur I. D. Sytin, launched the publishing house "Intermediary," located in a separate building on the Khamovniki grounds. It was Tolstoy's third attempt to promote literacy in Russia, and just as successful and important as the second one. It brought literature (and images) that were both high quality and cheap to an ever-expanding group of lower-class readers. Tolstoy remained involved with this project until the end of his life, and it continued to provide millions of cheap books and pamphlets for the masses until 1917. Maude reported in his biography that it helped inspire similar initiatives in England.

Its founders intended Intermediary to spread Tolstoy's new teaching, and he produced a series of stories with this in mind. They are all written in the tone and style developed in the 1870s for stories written for his primers and readers, and all of them benefit from Tolstoy's reading of folk literature. Many feature devils and angels, but these creatures function as metaphors about moral life rather than evidence of the supernatural. Some (A *Spark Neglected Burns the House*) illustrate proverbs, the way many stories from the 1870s do. They differ from the earlier stories because many of them lean more toward the ideal and symbolic, rather than the real. An example of this would be the legend *What People Live By*, written in 1881 but republished in Intermediary in 1885. In it, a shoemaker befriends a frozen, naked stranger he finds by a shrine on the road. Though the shoemaker and his wife do not learn this until the end, the stranger turns out to be a fallen angel whom God has punished for disobeying Him out of pity for the woman whose soul he was ordered to take. The angel is called home to God only after he has learned three truths related to God's mercy and the necessity of human suffering and mortality. (Another good example of this type of story would be *Two Old Men* [1885].) All the stories published in Intermediary illustrate principles proclaimed in Tolstoy's treatises of the period. Almost all feature a struggle between the animal and rational sides of the human soul. In all of them, one side prevails, and we see the consequences of this according to Tolstoy's psychology. The grimmest work published for the people was the play *The Power of Darkness*, which features the offstage murder by crushing of an infant and the poisoning of an older husband. Though intended by Tolstoy for the popular theater, it was published in both Intermediary and the collected works, because it speaks in Shakespearean tones of pathos to all classes. In 1888, it was performed to rave reviews in Paris at The Free Theatre of Director Andre Antoine; Emile Zola was one of its greatest admirers. Despite its naturalism, the play ends with the triumph of goodness and the sacred. Nikita, one of the three conspirators, publically confesses and takes upon himself all the guilt for both crimes. Not everyone liked the play. Reading it, Konstantin Pobedonostsev, advisor to Tsar Alexander III (and later to his son Nicholas II), Ober Curator of the Holy Synod, and a determined enemy of Tolstoy, "couldn't get over his horror." Censors forbade its performance, and it was staged in Russia only in 1895 when Tsar Nicholas II ascended the throne.

The works for the people can also reflect how much Tolstoy changed in the 1880s. A short story titled *How Much Land Does a Man Need?* (1886), for instance, relates how the peasant Pahom tries to buy land from the Bashkirs, so that he will not have to work so hard to make a living. A Bashkir chieftain offers to sell him for a fixed price as much land as he can circumnavigate by foot in a day. In the end, Pahom dies trying to maximize the acreage, and it turns out that he needs just the space necessary to hold his coffin. Tolstoy took the basics of the plot from Herodotus, and he set it within a completely folk milieu. Behind the scenes, the Devil manipulates the whole plot and triumphs in the end. At the same time, the story can be understood as a comment on Tolstoy's own experience in Bashkir lands and the property he acquired there. His Samara estate, to which he had devoted so much time and energy, is boiled down here to a cautionary tale about the dangers of human greed and overreach.

In the 1880s, Tolstoy began to be published abroad. Foreigners were introduced to his fiction and his treatises simultaneously, and this, of course, affected how they read the former. Starting then, many of his new works were banned in Russia or so heavily censored that they were practically unrecognizable. Many appeared abroad and in foreign languages before they were published in Russia. *What I Believe*, for instance, appeared first in Paris in 1885 as *Ma réligion*, in a translation by Tolstoy's friend L. D. Urusov. Later the same year, a shortened Russian version came out in the Russian émigré journal *General Affairs* in Geneva and then in book form in a Russian language press located in the same city, and founded by 1860s revolutionary immigrant M. K. Elpidin. Elpidin Press subsequently published many of Tolstoy's works. *What I Believe* did not appear in Russia until 1906 but, like Tolstoy's other banned or censored works, it circulated broadly in manuscript form. In 1897, when Chertkov was exiled from Russia for his work with sectarians, he founded the Free Word Press in England that published Russian language editions of Tolstoy's works and later, in 1900, its affiliate the Free Age Press that produced English editions of them.

As Tolstoy constructed his teaching in the 1880s, he began to focus attention on himself deliberately. In the non-fictional works discussed in this chapter, he created a persona that was part guru and part holy fool, part wise man and part repentant sinner. (A holy fool in the Russian Orthodox tradition is an eccentric person with a special connection to the sacred, often unconcerned with his physical well-being or respect for power.) Having read these works and others, people began to flock to visit Tolstoy in Moscow, and then at Yasnaya Polyana, which became a destination for pilgrims from all over the world. He tried to embody his own teaching in his personal image, as a model for good action, but also, in confessional writings, as human, all too human. He shared private issues and struggles even with strangers. An example of this is a long letter he wrote in 1882 to a young Christian revolutionary named M. A. Engelhardt, who had contacted Tolstoy out of the blue. In the letter to Engelhardt, he explained his ideals, his failure to live up to these, and his loneliness in the midst of his unsympathetic family. Perhaps uncomfortable with its intimacy, he did not send the letter, but he allowed Chertkov and others to read it, and it began to be circulated broadly. Subsequently, he wrote other seemingly private letters intended for public consumption, and also articles in the form of letters. This signaled his desire to connect directly—rather than indirectly through his fiction—with readers. Previously, he had guarded his privacy. The painting of him created by I. N. Kramskoy in 1873 is the very first image of the author produced for public consumption (for the Tretyakov Gallery in Moscow), and, so far as I know, the only famous one depicting him as an artist. All the others, starting in the 1880s, provide visual images of his new public persona. In his final years, he was painted, sculpted, and photographed many times.

Despite the government's attempts to muzzle Tolstoy through censorship, his fame as spiritual leader and social critic spread at home and abroad. In his public persona presented in both images and in his writings, Tolstoy became a role model for people all over the world. Tolstoyans in various countries formed colonies to live the life he recommended, and they acted in what they considered a Tolstoyan manner. Tolstoyanism, as practiced by a group, was always a contested notion, because its definition depended on the voice of conscience in each individual, and these voices disagreed among themselves. Furthermore, since Tolstoy opposed social hierarchies in general, it was difficult to create even the minimum hierarchy required for a commune. Therefore, many groups and individuals adopted his life of conscience, but participated in social causes important to them.

Not all in Tolstoy's life was doom, gloom, and battles in the family, even during the 1880s or later. Although he used his experience renovating Khamovniki in depicting the philistine life of Ivan Ilych, the time he spent in Moscow was in many ways fulfilling, and even crucial to his mission. While the master labored over his writings in a secluded corner on the second floor, the energetic Sofya oversaw the many activities of a household of 10 children and 10 or so employees. He was free to drop in on events and leave them as he wished. The Tolstoys hosted great artists, sculptors, writers, musicians, and public intellectuals of the time, and Tolstoy developed friendships with many of them. Daughter Tatyana was a gifted artist herself, and the house today is full of family portraits created by her and such artists as Nikolai Ge and I. E. Repin. Many musicians performed in private concerts there. Tolstoy, who loved music and often wept when it was played, enjoyed these events. At the same time as he was writing *The Kreutzer Sonata*, he also wrote a comedy called *The Fruits of Enlightenment*. It depicts a Moscow household of gentry and servants, and peasants who come to negotiate a business deal with the master. Though the play reflects themes from his treatises at the time—it satirizes the craze for spiritualism among the upper classes and contrasts the serious, hard-working life of the peasants with the empty, leisured one of the upper classes—it does not simply demonize the gentry or idealize the peasants. Tolstoy gave Tatyana permission to stage a family performance of the piece at Khamovniki during New Year's celebrations in 1889, and he thoroughly enjoyed it, laughing uproariously at some of the scenes. He reported in his diary that he was ashamed of taking delight in such gentry entertainment, but this did not prevent him from following the rehearsals closely and continuously altering the manuscript in response to them. The play itself, he remarked, was "not bad." Here and elsewhere, Tolstoyanism was a role he assumed and mostly believed in, but he could not be as strict a Tolstoyan as some of his ardent followers were. When he took up riding a bicycle in 1895, some of his supporters criticized that as undignified, but he continued to ride for two years. He often expressed guilt for doing what he wanted, but he did it anyway. While his followers had to obey the rules of his teaching, he could not always do so without losing that authenticity that was at the heart of his charisma as a teacher and, perhaps even more importantly, his genius as a writer. He had to remain free to acknowledge and respond to all his impulses and thoughts.

6. Tolstoy as Guru and Man in Later Life

Later in life, Tolstoy portrayed himself in public, as well as in his treatises and polemics, as a voice of reason (of the sort discussed above) who spoke for everyone rather than for single individuals, and urged each person to act for the general rather than personal good. As we have also mentioned, this persona was not godlike in his perfection; at times, Tolstoy confessed that he was prey to the same temptations that he condemned in others. At other times, the persona interacted uneasily with his late art.

The Kingdom of God is Within You, or Christianity Not as a Mystical Teaching, but as a New Understanding of Life (1890-93)

Tolstoy explained in the Preface to this long treatise that it grew out of readers' responses to *What I Believe*. Quakers from America had written him, for instance, agreeing with his pacifism and informing him that they had been conscientious objectors for more than 200 years. He had also heard from the son of prominent American abolitionist and social reformer William Lloyd Garrison about a declaration of non-resistance drawn up by his father over 50 years earlier, in 1838; Tolstoy included the declaration in *The Kingdom of God Is Within You*. The younger Garrison also told him about another American reformer, Adin Ballou, with whom Tolstoy then briefly corresponded until Ballou's death in 1890. In *The Kingdom of God Is Within You*, Tolstoy quoted extensively from Ballou's writings on non-resistance. From a German professor in Prague, he learned about the Christian pacifism of the 15th-century Bohemian spiritual leader Peter Chelcicky, and he quoted from Chelcicky's book *The Net of Faith*. Here and throughout *The Kingdom of God is Within You*, Tolstoy cited other authors and documents, foreign and Russian, as well. In his own mind, his non-fictional works had become a way to interact with like-minded people around the world and across time.

What Then Must We Do? had attacked the injustice and hypocrisy of the existing order. Now, in *The Kingdom of God is Within You*, Tolstoy attacked all governments as authoritarian, calling for non-violent civil disobedience, and especially refusal to serve in the military, to bring that order to an end. He declared that universal military service was an extreme form of violence used to coerce where the powerful could not convince, and if it were to be abolished, every rotten system based on it would collapse. Chapter 12 of this work provides vivid tableaus of the injustices and violence Tolstoy had witnessed in Russian society. These acts were committed by elites who, if they listened to the voice of reasonable consciousness in themselves, would reject their social roles as artificial and evil. Tolstoy again addressed the question of human freedom, arguing that most of our actions are based on habitual and unself-conscious assumptions. If we knew nothing of divine truth or all of it, we would not be free. But to the extent that we are self-conscious, we are in a transitional state with choices—free ones—to move toward truth or not. Thus, Tolstoy called for an "effort of the consciousness" by individuals—masters and slaves alike—to free themselves from hypocrisy. He assured his readers that, if this were to happen, the Kingdom of God, with equality and freedom for all and no necessity for government, would come into being. He attributed the fact that this new order had not yet been created to "hypnotism" of the masses by those who love power, preserving the status quo through false education and propaganda which had become easier to spread as communications and literacy improved. Through their enslavement of others, these elites had distanced themselves from the continuous hard labor necessary in nature for each individual to sustain life. Such labor moderated the passions, and when the elites had liberated themselves from it, the natural curb on excess by means of physical exertion no longer restrained them.

"Christianity and Patriotism" (1893)

Tolstoy considered war another impediment to the realization of a Christian world. He especially attacked the patriotism characteristic of the 1890s, which called for rivalries among nations. In this related essay from the period, Porfirii, an elderly Yasnaya Polyana peasant worn out by a lifetime of hard work, reacts with bewilderment to patriotic attacks on Germans by a wealthy French visitor. He doesn't see any difference between Russians like himself and Germans, saying the Germans should come to work with him on the land (Chapter 9). Earlier, however, Tolstoy acknowledged the effect of mass displays of patriotism on potential cannon fodder like this peasant, and even on himself. So (in Chapter 2), reading about a solemn reception of Russian sailors by their French allies, he is moved to tears, which he struggles to suppress. As a former soldier who sublimely described Russians at war in the Sevastopol sketches and in *War and Peace*, Tolstoy understood the power of such feelings. At one time, he had regarded them as expressive of an intimacy with others and an overcoming of selfishness that he desired. "Christianity and Patriotism" ferociously attacks patriotic feelings by reducing to mere rhetoric the language of patriotism that he himself had used earlier. In Chapter 12, he argued that patriotism, despite its power, is an artificial mood akin to drunkenness that, without the efforts of governments to stoke it, would soon vanish. And he claimed, once again, that if individuals rebelled against the tyranny of patriotic nationalism, then "real public opinion"–the "invincible force" of the conclusions of reasonable consciousness shared by all–would prevail (chapter 17).

Religious doctrine and social activism

To Tolstoy, the Kingdom of God was the political and social realization of Christian anarchism. While he certainly had experienced the old order with all its injustices, he could only imagine the new one. (He never lived among the dissenters whom he so admired and who, he thought, lived such a life.) Beyond trying unsuccessfully to convert his own family to Christian anarchism, he never actively participated in constructing a society based on its principles. He stood back even from his own followers in this regard, remaining a single voice consulting only his own conscience. Keeping his inner life healthy had, therefore, become an obsession with Tolstoy. In 1890, while working on *The Kingdom of God is Within You*, he wrote an article called "Why Do Men Stupefy Themselves?," in which he attacked drugs (including tobacco) and alcohol as conducive to crime because they mute the voice of conscience. This article contains the famous assertion (in Chapter 4) that the murderer Rodion Raskolnikov in Dostoevsky's 1866 novel *Crime and Punishment* was responsible for his crimes not as he was committing them, when he was acting like a machine, but when he was lying on his bed reflecting, and formulating the opinions that prompted and justified those crimes. Tolstoy strove now to be the personification of the voice of conscience. This does not mean that he was a hypocrite. Far from it! He did what that voice dictated, even when it seemed to contradict his own principles. On the other hand, he would not do what the voice counseled against, even if it meant not engaging in actions seemingly necessary to put his principles into practice.

By the 1880s and 1890s, Tolstoy had many followers at home and abroad. Tolstoyans came from all walks of life, but they all had in common their attraction to his teaching on conscience and non-resistance to evil. This idea inspired conscientious objectors, many of whom paid dearly for their actions. Utopian agricultural colonies based on Tolstoyan principles sprang up in Russia and in European countries, as well as the United States, South Africa, Japan, India, Palestine, and China. Among the most famous reformers indebted to Tolstoy's teaching were Jane Addams, William Jennings Bryan, and Mahatma Gandhi, but there were many, many others. However, the organizations which they founded or in which they participated could not be based on Tolstoyan principles alone, because, as mentioned in the previous chapter, these concepts mostly precluded political or even organized community actions. Tolstoyanism's main practical tenet, non-resistance to evil, proved useful later in the case of Gandhi's success in freeing India from British colonial rule. (In 1909, Gandhi wrote Tolstoy that the work which most inspired him was *The Kingdom of God is Within You*.) It is hard to see how such a policy would help in dealing with more brutal and fanatical oppressors, such as the Stalinists in the 20th century or terrorists in the 21st.

Tolstoy himself was distracted from his mission by an event, the deadly and widespread famine of 1891-92, which consumed much of his attention for two years. The famine was caused by a drought, and the peasant class lived under such extreme duress that it could not weather fluctuations of climate such as this one. The government was at least partly responsible for their state. After the emancipation, it had favored the interests of the gentry over the peasants, who had to buy their land rather than receive it outright. In many cases, transfers of land were delayed. As the government tried to industrialize and move toward a modern, capitalist economy, peasants had to pay very high taxes to finance changes like improved infrastructure, and they also paid very high indirect taxes on staples like vodka. The high consumer taxes forced them to sell their grain at low prices to merchants who then exported it. Additionally, the commune system so extolled by some of the intelligentsia discouraged the innovation needed to make agriculture productive. (Tolstoy himself was not a fan of the traditional Russian peasant commune [the *mir*], although he celebrated communal agricultural activities.) In 1873, he had been involved in famine relief work in Samara Province, and a letter he wrote to a Moscow newspaper about conditions there had raised almost 2 million roubles and 375 tons of grain in donations. Now, as famine raged in the Russian heartland, the Tolstoys united to save starving peasants, and tensions in the family eased. While Sofya stayed in Moscow with the four younger children and raised money for the cause there, Tolstoy and the five older ones visited ravaged areas and set up soup kitchens in them.

The Tsarist government underestimated and misreported the depths of the famine, and did little to address it. It even delayed a ban on grain exports. This made Tolstoy's actions glitter all the more brightly before a horrified and disenchanted Russian public. He emerged from the crisis with enormous prestige, while the government in the 1890s faced turmoil and criticism after a relatively tranquil previous decade. In 1898, Tolstoy engaged again in famine relief in districts nearby. Nonetheless, his convictions about the deep-rooted causes of peasant misery did not change, nor did he cease to criticize charitable, short-term efforts by civil society as a way of perpetuating the status quo. He wrote articles about the famine, alerting the public to the disaster and reporting on the best means to counter it. At the same time, in "On Hunger" (1891), he attacked the socio-political system which, in his opinion, was responsible for this catastrophe.

With *The Kingdom of God Is Within You*, the major planks of Tolstoy's religious philosophy and psychology were in place, and even though he continued to refine them, they did not change fundamentally in the last two decades of his life. For instance, a short book entitled *What is Religion and What is Its Essence?* (1901-02) is the most concise and clear definition of this essential subject, but introduces nothing drastically new to it. In the early 1890s, he read the writings of American political economist Henry George, and praised his single tax policy and rejection of private ownership of land. George's theories became the basis of Tolstoy's economic and social plan for Russia, but even in this case, he was relying on ideas developed in the 1880s. When in 1899-1900 he wrote *The Slavery of Our Times*, he was responding to the ideas of Karl Marx and socialism, but, as he explained at the beginning of this short book, his reactions led him directly back to the analysis and recommendations of *What Then Must We Do?* He called again for the rejection of all government, laws, and taxes, this time even those proposed by George. He reminded readers that conscience requires abstaining from any violence, including that advocated by revolutionaries. Tolstoy's attacks on the state and society grew more ferocious and extreme. Starting in the 1880s, the government and the church (really one and the same thing) feared his influence, and attacks on him began to be published.

Pacifism

Tolstoy's writings about the many wars and military actions of the last two decades of his life develop the practical implications of his teaching. True to his Christian anarchism, he rejected the usefulness of peace congresses and declarations like the Hague Conventions of 1899 and 1907. In "Carthago Delenda Est" (1898) and elsewhere, he argued that the way to end wars declared by governments is one man at a time, through draft resistance. By the time he wrote this work, Tolstoy was able to cite several cases of Tolstoyan conscientious resisters who had been punished or even died for refusing to serve in the army. Several times he wished that he, not those he had inspired, could be the one persecuted for this dissension. In "The End is Near" (1896), he predicted that their heroic stands of conscience heralded the end of the present world and the beginning of a new one. In "Patriotism or Peace" (1895-6), he attacked the patriotism that he believed was the driving force behind all the wars of the period. "Two Wars" (1898) contrasts the "pagan" Spanish-American War with the "holy" one waged against the Russian government by the sectarian Dukhobors, who refused to serve in the army. When King Umberto I of Italy was killed by an anarchist in 1900, Tolstoy wrote an article entitled "Thou Shalt Not

Kill!," in which he deplored the assassination because, he argued, it would change nothing; he also called in it for the rejection of all kings, emperors, and presidents whose main task was murder through wars. He followed this train of thought by condemning the Russo-Japanese War (1904-05) in "Bethink Yourselves!"

Radicalism at Home

In addition to his opposition to war, Tolstoy spoke out against revolution and social upheaval as the way to right wrongs in Russia. Revolutionaries began to appear in his fiction (in such works as *Resurrection* [1889-99] and *The Divine and Human* [1906]), portrayed as sympathetic in their desire for social justice but wrong-headed in their methods. After student disturbances and public demonstrations were repressed by the government in 1901, he helped lead the protests of civil society against this, penning a letter signed by many, and an article "To the Tsar and his Helpers," in which he called for reforms that he said would quell the violence. It was at this time that the Holy Synod of the Russian Orthodox Church excommunicated him. (It had been especially provoked by a scene in *Resurrection* depicting the Eucharist as cannibalism.) The international uproar in reaction to this move was deafening, and Tolstoy's prestige as the moral voice of Russian society once again soared. When the Revolution of 1905 broke out after Russia's humiliating defeat by the Japanese, all sides competed for his support. Preferring to keep his hands clean, he granted it to none, and wrote pamphlets like *The End of an Age* (1905) in which he argued that the present upheaval was a spiritual one, ushering in the changes he had advocated for so long. He declined to back those who wanted to replace absolutism with a constitutional monarchy; Tolstoy's loyal but independent-minded follower Aylmer Maude criticized him for this in his biography. In one of his most influential articles, "I Cannot Be Silent" (1908), Tolstoy denounced capital punishment. But he also criticized the revolutionaries. In three articles written in 1906 ("A Letter to a Chinese," "The Significance of the Russian Revolution," and "An Address to the Russian People: to the Government, to the Revolutionaries, and to the Masses"), he condemned them—so much so that Chertkov urged him to moderate his tone—and argued against the suitability of industrialization and Western democracy for Russia.

Personal Life

The Tolstoy of the treatises was stridently dogmatic. Even though he occasionally conceded, as he did at the end of *The Slavery of Our Times*, that not everyone could follow all his principles all at once, he urged readers to go as far as they possibly could. In an 1896 letter to American Tolstoyan Ernest Howard Crosby, he defended non-resistance to evil, even if it meant not killing a thief to save a child. His life was not strictly consistent in this way, and this duality was part of his attraction. For instance, Tolstoy's official position on famine relief, first expressed in *What Is To Be Done?*, was that charitable work by the upper classes merely perpetuated and even encouraged the status quo. However, his old friend and neighbor Ivan Raevsky convinced him that he had to get involved in the famine crisis, even if it meant contravening his principles. Chertkov, on the other hand, who was more principled and hard-hearted, advised Tolstoy against participating. In another example, when the Boer War began in 1899, Tolstoy had to suppress an urge to support the Boers against the British. And critical though he was of the Russian side in the Russo-Japanese War, he confessed that he felt like volunteering to fight, and he followed Russian defeats with dismay. He did not hide these impulses and contradictions. On the contrary, he regarded them as proof of his lack of dogmatism. Through them, he modeled the way we juggle our different impulses, and at times contradict ourselves while trying to do the right thing.

In 1891, Tolstoy publicly renounced copyright to all his works published after 1881, and in 1892, he signed over all his property to his wife and children. In 1895, a catastrophe befell the Tolstoys. Ivan (Vanya), their beloved youngest child, died at age seven of scarlet fever. Biographer Lydia Gromova-Opulskaya believed that neither parent ever recovered from this blow. His thoughts focused on death, Tolstoy tried to react stoically, while Sofya was inconsolable, even unhinged. She turned to music for comfort, and began to go out frequently, dressed to kill, to concerts and the theater. She developed a bizarre crush on a frequent houseguest, pianist S. I. Taneev, that lasted at least four years. Although the relationship was platonic—Taneev was homosexual—Tolstoy was intensely jealous and threatened to leave home. The death of Vanya temporally drew the couple together, but they remained spiritually and intellectually far apart. Tolstoy's two older daughters worshipped their father and took their mother's place as his loyal intimates. When they married—Marya in 1897 and Tatyana in 1899—it was a great blow to their father, who had been ungraciously jealous of their attachment to all the men who had courted them. He remained close to them, but felt bereft without their undivided attention. All the while, tensions between Sofya and the Tolstoyans boiled, though they eased somewhat when Chertkov left for England in 1897.

In his 60s, despite occasional indispositions, Tolstoy remained vigorous and athletic. In 1899, however, he fell seriously ill, first of malaria and then pneumonia. As part of his cure, the family moved to Gaspra in Crimea, to a palace lent to them by Countess Sofya Panina. Although he survived, he did not regain his earlier physical stamina and suffered other spells of illness in his final decade. His brother Sergey died in 1904, and—an especially hard blow—his daughter Marya in 1905.

With the liberalization that followed the 1905 revolution, Chertkov was allowed to return to Russia. He visited in summers, and in 1908 he began to live full time in a house owned by Tolstoy's daughter,

Aleksandra, who sided with him, near Yasnaya Polyana. The stage was set for the showdown between him and Sofya, who was now desperately trying to protect her legacy, her children's inheritance, and her access to her husband. The duelling photographs taken by the two rivals, each trying to document their closeness to Tolstoy, are evidence of her competition with Chertkov. By 1908, though he and Sofya had shared their diaries for their entire married life, Tolstoy was keeping a second one secret from her. When he finally left home in the middle of the night in October 1910, accompanied only by his personal physician, it was because Sofya had been rummaging through his papers in his study without his permission. When she learned that he was gone, she tried to drown herself. Her behavior in Tolstoy's final years was impossible, and she was ashamed of it later. Still, Chertkov must be blamed for relentlessly stirring the stew of marital discord. In the mid-1920s, Maxim Gorky wrote a reminiscence about Sofya to counter a damning one by Chertkov. Though Gorky confessed that he had been no admirer of her nor she of him, he praised Sofya's dedication to her family and her husband, her efforts over decades to shield him from outside unpleasantness, and especially her remarkable organizational skills on display at Gaspra, where he had visited.

Then there is Tolstoy's own explanation of his relations with his wife in his unfinished, posthumously published play *The Light Shines in Darkness* (1896-97, 1900, possibly 1902). The main character, Nikolay Ivanovich, tries to apply his Tolstoyan principles to his own life, and that of his family and friends. He wants to give almost all his property to peasants, and till the land he keeps himself, and he protests the prosecution of peasants who cut wood in his forests. (Tolstoy and Sofya clashed over such matters more than once.) Though he sees that everyone is suffering as a result of his new ideas, and he tenderly loves his family, Nikolay remains committed to his truths. His wife, though she loves and wants to follow him, cannot do so because of the consequences for the material well-being of their children. For Tolstoy, this was a tragedy, an unavoidable clash between the natural animal love of mothers for their children and the spiritual love of all of those in touch with God.

Maude's judgment on these matters is also insightful. With Sofya looking after his personal needs and Chertkov the public requirements of Tolstoyanism, Tolstoy was freed from all practical responsibilities. Taking out chamber pots, making shoes, or working on the harvest (especially when choosing when and if to do so) was not all that time-consuming, and he did not involve himself in the machinations of Tolstoyan communes. He certainly knew Sofya's and Chertkov's shortcomings—Sofya's behavior, including suicide attempts, is anticipated in scenes of female jealousy in *Anna Karenina*; he was also aware of Chertkov's imperiousness—but Tolstoy loved and needed them both. His task was to be himself, both to enact that role and, equally important, to remain open to the dictates, whatever they might be, of his inner life and conscience. Contradictory though he may have been, ornery and overly dogmatic at times, I cannot think of a single instance in his life when Tolstoy consciously schemed on his own behalf or kowtowed to others. His aristocratic integrity was phenomenal, and a main source of his appeal down to this day.

Even amid all the misery, there were still joyful moments. Yasnaya Polyana and Khamovniki were full of music and guests. Tolstoy laughed and joked, danced the mazurka, and wept at concerts staged for him at home. In Crimea, he reminisced about his time in Sevastopol, and enjoyed the beautiful scenery and weather. He bragged to Gorky about his youthful libido, and had long, heartfelt conversations with Anton Chekhov. When he returned to central Russia from the south, his doctors, to his relief, forbade him to winter any longer in Moscow. It was at this time that his study at Yasnaya Polyana was moved from downstairs to the second floor next to his bedroom, where it still is today. In 1904, Slovenian doctor and follower Dushan Makovitsky became his devoted live-in physician. Not wanting to disturb the intimacy of life at Yasnaya Polyana, but considering every word uttered by Tolstoy to be significant for posterity, Makovitsky scribbled the master's comments in a notebook he carried in his pocket. Even after his illness, Tolstoy went on long walks summer and winter, and reported on the beauty of nature. He played chess and rode his favorite mount, Délire. His love for Sofya bubbled beneath the surface and flared up from time to time. The two of them delighted in their grandchildren, especially the late, unexpected only child (a daughter) of the 41-year-old Tatyana. In 1906-07, he returned to teaching children on his estate.

The tensions in his personal life did not diminish Tolstoy's immense public influence in the last decade of his life. Pilgrims visited and wrote to him from all over the world. Wherever he traveled, crowds gathered to cheer him. In Russia, he was a modern-day Ilya Muromets, a valiant knight from a Russian legend, and the state feared him like fire. Spies reported on his every movement.

7. Art and Aesthetics in the Late Period

As a prophet and role-model, the later Tolstoy criticized art that privileged beauty and pleasure over ethics. (He targeted writers like the decadent French poet Charles Baudelaire.) When he gave into his own desire to write fiction that did not simply illustrate his teachings, he felt guilty. Nonetheless, he still produced such fiction during the last two decades of his life. While his own art always had a moral purpose, it did not present life in black and white terms. In *What Is Art?*, his most authoritative statement on the subject, he defined it as follows.

> To call up in oneself a feeling once experienced and, having called it up in oneself, to transmit it by means of movements, lines, colors, sounds, images expressed in words so that others will experience the very same feeling: the activity of art consists in this. Art is a human activity that consists in one person consciously, using certain external signs, transmitting to others feelings experienced by him, and other people becoming infected by these feelings and experiencing them.

Depending on the feelings summoned, Tolstoy conceded, art can be good or bad; in this sense, it is sub-moral. In its essence, however, it is fundamentally good because it unites people, and the best art, according to Tolstoy, unites all people in brotherhood. He distinguished between "universal" and "religious" art. The first is experienced by all, while the second conveys the highest religious feeling of the culture and time in which it is produced. In his own time, he stated, this was Christian. His example of the first type in his own art is his story *A Prisoner of the Caucasus* and of the second—*God Sees the Truth, but Waits*; both these stories were published in 1872 in his first primer. He rejected all his other works as inferior to these two. The difference between them, he said, was the universality of attachment to one's own in the former, as opposed to the highest religious mandate expressed in the latter as forgiveness even of one's enemies. Though Tolstoy did not discuss or give examples of morally bad art, it would be the kind that infects others with such feelings as hate, love of power, superiority over others, desire for revenge, or lust. He also did not explore why the artist might want to infect others. As we have seen in this book, in Tolstoy's case at least, the reasons were related more to his own neediness than to his goals as a moral actor. So when he continues in his later period to want to transmit his feelings to others, he feels guilty about this.

The range of Tolstoy's artistic production during this time was very broad, and he was not ashamed of all of it. On one end of the spectrum, the distinction between his non-fictional tracts and his art is somewhat artificial, because his most powerful tool even in his polemics is his artistic genius. A good example is "I Cannot Be Silent," in which, imagining himself at one point dangling from a noose, he infected his readers with the feelings of those being hanged, so as to express the full horror of the experience and shift public opinion, one reader at a time, against capital punishment. Tolstoy's tracts are full of similes of the sort he admired in Homer's *Iliad* and *Odyssey*. This technique is closely related to parables, which he also loved and wrote. Some of these, like *Three Parables* (1894-95), come with explanations of their meaning, but most have their moral built in. He also continued to write edifying stories, often borrowing them from folktales and legends of various cultures. In 1903, for instance, he contributed three such tales (*Esarhaddon*, *Three Questions*, and *Work, Death and Illness*) to an anthology raising money for the victims of the anti-Jewish pogrom in the city of Kishinev. In this last decade of his life, he also worked on what he called a Circle of Reading (as well as a spin-off for children). It consisted of daily readings from materials taken from all over the world. In addition to compiling this content and translating and rewriting many of the entries, he contributed some original works to it (for instance, *Berries* [1905] and *Divine and Human* [1906]). Even though masterful, these didactic stories remained subordinate to his teachings. Another late work in this mode is *Alyosha the Pot* (1905, published 1911). It describes the life and death of a kind of holy fool who serves others and accepts the injustices of his master without complaint. Tolstoy's guilty pleasures were those in which his artistic imagination took the lead. (They include *Master and Man* and *Hadji Murat*, discussed below.) When this happened, he criticized himself for indulging in fiction, or things that were untrue.

Resurrection (1889-99)

Making an exception to his policy of accepting no money for his late works, Tolstoy published his last novel for profit to fund the emigration of the sectarian Dukhobors to Canada. Prince Dimitri Nekhlyudov seduces Katyusha Maslova, a ward of his aunt. Unbeknownst to him, she becomes pregnant, gives up the baby, and turns to prostitution. Years later, while a jury member in a murder trial, Nekhlyudov recognizes Maslova as the accused. As he tries to help her and then follows her to Siberia when she is convicted, the novel broadens into a depiction and indictment of every aspect of the Russian criminal justice system. Nekhlyudov's education in the dictates of reasonable consciousness is complete when Maslova, herself a changed woman, turns down his marriage proposal. In the course of the novel, both are "resurrected" to their best selves. The novel ends rather abruptly, with Nekhlyudov pondering his future and reading Tolstoy's favorite passages from the Gospels, including the Sermon on the Mount.

Tolstoy was dissatisfied with this work because it focused on the upper classes and was intended for them. Readers today might criticize it for another reason: that it is excessively satirical in its portrayal of Russian society, and unforthcoming about Nekhlyudov's life after his transformation into a Tolstoyan. Tolstoy may have had this last problem in mind when he wrote in a diary entry in 1900 that "I want terribly to write something artistic, and not dramatic, but epic—a continuation of *Resurrection*: the peasant life of Nekhlyudov." There is no detailed account in any of Tolstoy's works of a gentryman who becomes a commoner, and two who try to do this—Olenin in *The Cossacks* and Levin in *Anna Karenina*—fail. The narrator of *Resurrection* created a problem in it that Sofya identified and that may have troubled Tolstoy: the love affair of Nekhlyudov and Maslova is depicted as too erotic, too positive. Here the author may have let his artistic imagination influence him. A work that successfully highlights a form of spiritual love, and one written right after *Resurrection*, is the play *The Living Corpse* (1900). It is a tragedy in which the hero tries to do the right thing by faking suicide so that his wife can marry a better man, but he ends up having to shoot himself when it is discovered that he is still alive.

Master and Man (1895)

A merchant and his manservant get lost in a snowstorm as they travel to clinch a business deal. The merchant dies, but he saves the servant's life by lying on top of him until rescuers arrive in the morning. Reduced to its plot in this way—I leave out various complications—this short story sounds like one of Tolstoy's works for the masses. It is greater than any of them, however, because of its psychological sophistication. The merchant's point of view (as well as those of the servant and even the horse) is depicted with unerring veracity. When critic Richard Gustafson called *Master and Man* the most perfect of Tolstoy's works, he was referring to how the psychological, material, symbolic, and even allegoric elements all work harmoniously together in it. Why then was Tolstoy uneasy about writing it? Once again, I suspect that it was precisely its artistic perfection that made him uncomfortable. Especially problematic for his late theories was the way the story justifies the sacrifice of the merchant. By his final act, he both submits himself to the master of all (God), and confirms his own status as a master among men, while the manservant does not feel the same obligation toward the horse, though he does attempt, unsuccessfully, to save its life.

Hadji Murat (1896-1904)

An Avar warrior (Avars are an ethnic group native to the Caucasus), defects to the Russians in 1851 and then is killed in 1852 trying to escape. This true story, which Tolstoy heard while he was serving in the Caucasus, became the basis of his late epic. It is framed by an explanation of how this short novel came to be written. A first-person narrator is walking through plowed fields when he comes upon a sturdy thistle called a "Tatar." It alone has survived the plowing. When the narrator tries to pick its flower, the Tatar resists. Once placed in the narrator's bouquet, the thistle flower seems diminished. The strength and struggle of the Tatar remind the narrator of Hadji Murat's story, which he then constructs through his "memory and imagination." The work ends with a sentence comparing the thistle with the dying warrior, hacked and shot by his Russian pursuers. But if the frame narrative is an allegory of the cruelties of civilization, the inserted narrative becomes a full-fledged psychological portrait of Hadji Murat, which escapes the confines of the framing allegory. And while everything in the work is generalized into an epic, it is loaded with personal meaning for Tolstoy. He is the man in the frame gathering a bouquet as he routinely did on his walks at Yasnaya Polyana. Through Hadji Murat's experience, he imagines a heroic death for himself. He places his younger self in the work as the Russian officer Butler, with his noble intentions, his gambling, and his womanizing. As in Homer's *Iliad*, the incident related is part of a greater war; but unlike the wrath of Achilles, Hadji Murat's story does not affect the course of the war in any way. Instead, Hadji Murat demonstrates how to live and die in a situation over which the individual has no ultimate control. Broadening out from his personal fate, the work, mixing historical and fictional characters as needed, represents Tolstoy's final verdict on the Russian expansionist wars in the Caucasus in which he took part. His satire does not turn men into incomprehensible monsters. Even the negative portrayal of Nicholas I shows how the Tsar excuses his own deeds because he knows they are criminal. The omniscient narrator rarely comments. Instead, readers must juxtapose and compare the individual parts and scenes of the work so as to understand the whole. (The technique, which goes back to *War and Peace*, is strikingly cinematographic.) Yes, the conclusions we are invited to draw are Tolstoyan, but we can draw them or not, as we wish. The work is complex, multi-layered, and, like the title character, not simply subordinated to Tolstoy's late teaching. Hadji Murat is a religious man—his name indicates that he has taken the pilgrimage to Mecca (the hajj) required of all Muslims—but also a product of his warrior culture. When his luck runs out, and he must face death, he has no epiphany turning him into a Tolstoyan; he dies as a hero at peace with himself. He is nobler and more attractive than Prince Dimitri Nekhlyudov. So Tolstoy's last great work of literature implicitly undermines his later teaching in a way that may have troubled him.

8. Conclusion and Legacy

One of the secrets of Tolstoy's genius was his grounding in both Enlightenment and post-Enlightenment thought. In his late treatises, he called upon us to Be Reasonable, arguing that we are only true to our better selves when we act reasonably in the broadest sense of the term. At the same time, he remained throughout his life true to his belief that feeling precedes reason in human beings. In this respect, as in so many other cases, he adhered to Rousseau's doctrines. But Tolstoy was not willing to follow the consequences of Rousseau's correction of Enlightenment thought that led through Friedrich Nietzsche to 20th-century thinkers like Martin Heidegger. When he encountered Nietzsche in the late period—he discussed the German philosopher in "Religion and Morality," for instance—he recognized him as a great thinker who exposed the contradiction in secular rationalist ethics, which cannot succeed in arguing for a form of goodness that does not reward the individual. Tolstoy, by contrast, was a post-Kantian who relied on feeling rather than reason for access to a moral and reasonable universal truth necessary for ethics, and emanating from what—in the same passage from "Religion and Morality"—he called the "will of God." In his treatises, he argued that feeling and reason coincided with reasonable consciousness—the conduit to that will in the soul. Only if we heed that will can we escape the leaky boat of our mortal selves. His fiction illustrates both the ideals he espoused and the way we, as mere humans, fall short of them. My strongest criticism of Tolstoy is that he believed too much in human goodness, and did not confront the evil in human nature to the extent that, say, Dostoevsky did. Tolstoy knew about such evil—he depicted it in *The Kreutzer Sonata*, for instance—but he considered it a sickness rather than a "normal" state. His defense of virtue and goodness as something to which all human beings, even evil ones, aspire for themselves, is powerful. But can we be good in the face of monstrous injustice or will we react with anger and vengeance? Some of his late works—an example already mentioned would be the title character in the story *Alyosha the Pot*—depict saintly figures who forgive their enemies. In *Divine and Human* (1905), the Christian Anatoly Svetlogub pardons the hangman who executes him, while the revolutionary Ignaty Mezhenitsky hangs himself from anger and despair. Readers must decide for themselves which character is more psychologically convincing. Here and elsewhere, Tolstoy tried to show that even the greatest villains can't look their victims in the eye.

As a thinker, Tolstoy was a romantic shaped—or limited—by Enlightenment principles. But the author of fiction who loved analysis and categorizing dreamt up his works of fiction while in a state between waking and sleeping, and the insights he had in that state are not sacrificed in his masterworks to didactic moralizing. One of his favorite words was "simplicity," in Russian, *prostota*, which he often equated with goodness, though spontaneity would be a better overall definition of it. So, for instance, when he wrote in *War and Peace* that the main battle at Borodino went on "in the most simple, artless manner" (Volume 3, Part 2, Chapter 33), he meant that men were killing each other and dying without pretensions or plans. But the fictional worlds he created were not simple ones.

Because human beings and their environment are so complex, we are all different, and no one could show this better than Tolstoy; yet we all have the same nature, and this allows us to understand one another. In his later life, his quest for intimacy took the form of imagining not only his treatises, but also his fiction as letters to readers across space and time. I mention above that ostensibly private letters circulated widely and were in fact intended as general statements. (From the time of his marriage, his diary functioned in the same way.) The letter-article also became an important genre for him. "Patriotism or Peace," "To the Tsar and his Helpers," "A Letter to a Chinese," "and "An Address to the Russian People: to the Government, to the Revolutionaries, and to the Masses" are examples of how he expressed his thoughts in letter form. He defined *Resurrection* as "a general letter to all." This comment connected the narrator to the author of many of the late non-fictional works, but also reminds us that connection with readers underlies Tolstoy's need to write. In this sense, his artistic work is confessional, and not subordinated to any dogma, even his own. He shared his feelings with others, and by infecting them with those feelings, he and his readers become one, if only momentarily.

Having left home in 1910, Tolstoy fell ill while on a train, and because he lingered a few days at the station of Astapovo, journalists had time to gather there, and his death and subsequent funeral became one of the first worldwide media events. The New York Times published an obituary (sent by telegraph) on the day of his death (see http://www.nytimes.com/learning/general/onthisday/bday/0828.html [accessed 10/16/2016]). His legacy since then has been complex, and even contradictory. Tolstoy was both a pacifist and the greatest war writer of modern times. He was a Christian who tried to bridge the divide between reason and revelation. In his later years, he denounced revolutionary violence, yet also condemned in the thundering tone of an Old Testament prophet the injustice of government and therefore implicitly encouraged its overthrow. He preached love, but found very little of it in his family or society. He was a believer in universal brotherhood, whose novel *War and Peace* is a founding document of modern Russian nationalism. Author Vasily Grossman carried it with him as a frontline journalist covering World War II, and it inspired his great epic *Life and Fate* about the pivotal battle of Stalingrad. The official Soviet Tolstoy was Lenin's "mirror of the Russian Revolution," while Tolstoyans were ruthlessly persecuted as enemies of the state. Although in later life Tolstoy wore a peasant blouse so identified with him that it was called a *Tolstovka*, he was an aristocrat to the marrow of his bones for whom honor and dignity were all-important. A subtle explorer of the human soul, he influenced modernist writers like Marcel Proust and James Joyce, and yet he has been both praised and criticized as fundamentally didactic. Such diverse writers as Anton Chekhov, Boris Pasternak, Romain Rolland,

Thomas Mann, and Ernest Hemingway acknowledged his impact on them. Even though as a thinker Tolstoy was eclectic, his writings, both fictional and non-fictional, have influenced great philosophers like Ludwig Wittgenstein. Over time, his image seemed to change, too. Whereas during the Soviet period, he stood among the pantheon of great Russian writers, today, because of his radical politics and his attack on the Russian Orthodox Church, the regime has somewhat distanced itself from him. He may become once again a spokesman for dissenters, as he was during his lifetime.

The fact that Tolstoy is susceptible to many different interpretations helps explain his enduring and still widespread popularity. Despite his insistence on simplicity, he is satisfyingly complex, and his various readers find and focus on different elements of this complexity. His method of writing fiction allows them to do this. Yet to appreciate him fully, readers must navigate the labyrinth of his thought through the different scenes and characters that make up his works. Only then can they immerse themselves in Tolstoy's world and stitch the parts of that world together. The results do not explain everything, but challenge us in a way that few writers do to face the mysteries of "reality."

Sources

All translations from Tolstoy in this book follow the Academy edition of his works, *Polnoe sobranie sochinenii* (90 vols; Gosudarstvennoe izdatel'stvo "Khudozhestvennaia literatura," 1928-1958). All translations unless otherwise noted in this book are mine, though I consult other translations for best usage in fashioning my own. Amongst older translations, despite mistakes, I especially like those by Louise and Aylmer Maude and by Constance Garnett: the Maudes for their closeness to Tolstoy's tone, and Garnett for her subtle English. I have gathered information about Tolstoy's life from many places, but the most important sources are the fundamental biographical works in Russian by N. N. Gusev and L. D. Gromova-Opulskaya.

Russian is written in the Cyrillic alphabet, and there is no universally accepted way of transliterating Russian words into the Latin alphabet. Thus arises the vexed issue of how to render names, places, and the like into English. In this book where there is a common spelling or version of a word—Moscow, for instance, rather than Moskva, or names ending in 'y' rather than 'ii' (Dostoevsky rather than Dostoevskii)—I use it. Otherwise, I have chosen the form of transliteration that makes it easiest for English speakers to pronounce words.

Suggested Reading

In what follows, I mention only works available in English, and I limit myself to books only even though there are many wonderful articles about Tolstoy.

Translations

In addition to the many translations into English of Tolstoy's fiction, there are also translations, most of them quite old and some more accurate than others, of his treatises and articles about morality, religion, pedagogy, and war. Translations by Louise and Aylmer Maude are available on the internet. R. F. Christian has translated selections of Tolstoy's letters (Athlone Press, 1978) and his diaries (Athlone Press and Scribner Press, 1985). Bob Blaisdell's edited volume *Tolstoy as Teacher: Leo Tolstoy's Writings on Education* (Teachers and Writers, 2000) provides samples of Tolstoy's pedagogical writing. Over the last twenty years, Andrew Donskov has published a great deal of primary material related to Tolstoy.

Biographies

Aylmer Maude published a two-volume biography of Tolstoy that came out in 1908-1912, and then in a revised version with Oxford University Press in 1930 (*The Life of Tolstoy*). The latest reprint of it is from 1987, and the first part of it is online. Maude both admires Tolstoy and criticizes his politics from a very English point of view. Victor Shklovsky's *Lev Tolstoy* (1967; Progress Publishers,

1978) makes a strong case for Tolstoy as a debunker and "defamiliarizer." A.N. Wilson's *Tolstoy* (W. W. Norton & Co., 1988) is outstanding for its insights into the creative history of Tolstoy's works, and also for its measured account of the relations between Tolstoy and his wife. *Tolstoy. A Russian Life* by Rosamund Bartlett (Houghton Mifflin Harcourt, 2011) has made detailed use of the Russian sources mentioned above, and focuses on Tolstoy within the Russian context. (Bartlett's recent translation of *Anna Karenina* is also excellent.) William Nickell's *The Death of Tolstoy: Russia on the Eve, Astapovo Station, 1910* (Cornell UP, 2010) tells the story of Tolstoy's final days and death as well as the reaction of family and society to them.

Bibliography and More

Because Tolstoy led such a long life and wrote so much, I have had to focus on him, and say less than I might like about his milieu and especially those who influenced him, and by whom he was influenced. For secondary sources on this and other subjects, see David R. and Melinda A. Egan, eds. *Leo Tolstoy: An Annotated Bibliography of English Language Sources to 1978* (Scarecrow Press, 1979) and their *Leo Tolstoy: an annotated bibliography of English language sources from 1978 to 2003* (Scarecrow Press, Inc., 2005). **Tolstoy Studies Journal** has been a source of new criticism and bibliography since its founding in 1988. The journal has an invaluable website with old issues online and many other resources, including a picture gallery that can supplement this book. See http://www.tolstoy-studies-journal.com/.

Russian Perspectives

Three edited volumes—A. V. Knowles' edited volume *Tolstoy: The Critical Heritage* (Routledge and Kegan Paul Ltd., 1978), Henry Gifford's *Leo Tolstoy: A Critical Anthology* (Penguin Books, 1971), and Boris Sorokin's *Tolstoy in Prerevolutionary Criticism* (Ohio State University Press, 1979)—include critical materials that go back to Tolstoy's lifetime. Poet and intellectual D. S. Merezhkovsky's *Tolstoi as Man and Artist. With an Essay on Dostoevski* (1902; Scholarly Press, 1970) and Marxist and social Democrat Maxim Gorky's *Reminiscences of Tolstoy, Chekhov, and Andreyev* (Viking Press, 1959) give very different late Russian empire accounts of Tolstoy as a man, writer, and thinker. Essays by pessimist and existentialist philosopher Leo Shestov in *Dostoevsky, Tolstoy, and Nietzsche* (Ohio UP, 1969) and *In Job's Balances: On the Sources of the Eternal Truths* (1929; Ohio UP, 1975) study Tolstoy from a post-Nietzschean perspective. The formalist school of Russian criticism from the early Soviet Union is represented by a series of seminal books by Boris Eikhenbaum. These include *The Young Tolstoy* (1922; Ardis, 1972), *Tolstoy in the Sixties* (1928; Ardis, 1982), and *Tolstoy in the Seventies* (1931; Ardis, 1982). *On Psychological Prose* (1971; Princeton University Press, 1991) by Eikhenbaum's student Lydia Ginzburg is a must-read for those interested in Tolstoy's psychological realism.

English Language Criticism

Outstanding older books include Aylmer Maude's *Tolstoy and His Problems* (Funk and Wagnalls Company, 1904, available in the Internet Archive), Isaiah Berlin's *The Hedgehog and the Fox: An Essay on Tolstoy's View of History* (1953; Simon and Shuster, 1970), George Steiner's *Tolstoy or Dostoevsky: An Essay in the Old*

Criticism (Vintage Books, 1961), R. F. Christian's *Tolstoy's "War and Peace"* (Clarendon Press, 1962), John Bayley's *Tolstoy and the Novel* (The Viking Press, 1966), Elisabeth Stenbock-Fermor's *The Architecture of Anna Karenina: A History of its Structure, Writing, and Message* (Peter de Bidder Press, 1975), and Edward Wasiolek's *Tolstoy's Major Fiction* (University of Chicago Press, 1978). Richard F. Gustafson's *Leo Tolstoy: Resident and Stranger: A Study in Fiction and Theology* (Princeton UP, 1986) has been immensely and deservedly influential, as have Gary Saul Morson's *Hidden in Plain View: Narrative and Creative Potentials in 'War and Peace'* Stanford UP, 1986), Amy Mandelker's *Framing Anna Karenina: Tolstoy, the Woman Question and the Victorian Novel* (The Ohio State UP, 1993), and Kathryn B. Feuer's *The Genesis of War and Peace* (Cornell UP, 1996). Among my own books, I recommend two monographs, *Tolstoy's Art and Thought, 1847-1880* (Princeton UP, 1993) and *Consequences of Consciousness: Turgenev, Dostoevsky, Tolstoy* (Stanford UP, 2007) as well as two edited volumes, *The Cambridge Companion to Tolstoy* (Cambridge UP, 2002) and (with Rick McPeak) *Tolstoy on War: Narrative Art and Historical Truth in 'War and Peace'* (Cornell UP, 2012). Recent excellent publications include Jeff Love's *The Overcoming of History in 'War and Peace'* (Rodopi, 2004), Gary Saul Morson's *'Anna Karenina' in Our Time: Seeing More Wisely* (Yale UP, 2007), Inessa Medzhibovskaya's *Tolstoy and the Religious Culture of his Time. A Biography of a Long Conversion, 1845-1887* (Lexington Books, 2008), Andrew D. Kaufman's *Understanding Tolstoy* (The Ohio State UP, 2011), Justin Weir's *Leo Tolstoy & the Alibi of Narrative* (Yale UP, 2011), John Burt Foster's *Transnational Tolstoy: Between the West and the World* (Bloomsbury, 2013), Charlotte Alston's *Tolstoy and his Disciples: The History of a Radical International Movement* (I. B. Tauris, 2014), Irina Paperno's *Who, What am I?: Tolstoy Struggles to Narrate the Self* (Cornell UP, 2014) and Liza Knapp's *Anna Karenina and Others: Tolstoy's Labyrinth of Plots* (The University of Wisconsin Press, 2016). For those interested in media studies, Michael Denner's and Lorna Fitzsimmons' recent edited volume *Tolstoy on*

Screen (Northwestern UP, 2014) offers a comprehensive survey of screen adaptations of Tolstoy's works.

About the Author

Donna Tussing Orwin is Professor of Russian Literature in the Department of Slavic Languages and Literatures at the University of Toronto. She is the author of *Tolstoy's Art and Thought, 1847-1880* and *Consequences of Consciousness: Turgenev, Dostoevsky, Tolstoy*. She also edited *The Cambridge Companion to Tolstoy* and *Tolstoy Studies Journal*. A member of the Royal Society of Canada and recipient of the Pushkin Medal for her work in disseminating Russian culture, Orwin has helped organize conferences in Russia, Canada, and the United States.

A Word from the Publisher

Thank you for reading *Simply Tolstoy*!

If you enjoyed reading it, we would be grateful if you could help others discover and enjoy it too.

Please review it with your favorite book provider such as Amazon, BN, Kobo, Apple Books, or Goodreads, among others.

Again, thank you for your support and we look forward to offering you more great reads.

www.ingramcontent.com/pod-product-compliance
Lightning Source LLC
Chambersburg PA
CBHW021153080526
44588CB00008B/317